TLC

Talking
Listening
Connecting

D0106773

Paul M. Rosen, Ph.D.

ALPHA

A Pearson Education Company

International Standard Book Number: 0-02-864276-7
Library of Congress Catalog Card Number: 2001095856

04 03 02   8 7 6 5 4 3 2 1

Interpretation of the printing code: The rightmost number of the first series of numbers is the year of the book's printing; the rightmost number of the second series of numbers is the number of the book's printing. For example, a printing code of 02-1 shows that the first printing occurred in 2002.

Printed in the United States of America

Publisher: Marie Butler-Knight
Product Manager: Phil Kitchel
Managing Editor: Jennifer Chisholm
Senior Acquisitions Editor: Randy Ladenheim-Gil
Development Editor: Lynn Northrup
Production Editor: Katherin Bidwell
Copy Editor: Amy Borrelli
Cover Designer: Trina Wurst
Book Designer: Trina Wurst
Production: Angela Calvert, Svetlana Dominguez, Natashia Rardin

Contents

Introduction

"What would you like to play today?" I asked, even though I already knew what she would answer.

"I want to play Sorry."

"Okay, we'll play Sorry for a while," I said, "but how about we play with the dollhouse after we play one game of Sorry?"

"No, I don't want to play with the dollhouse. I just want to play Sorry."

Her name was Marisa, and she was my seven-year-old "patient." She had dark brown hair and freckles. I still remember her even though it has been over 20 years since she was in my office. We met for eight sessions, and we never did anything but play Sorry. Despite my efforts to get her to play something else or to talk about the reason her mother brought her to see me, I could not get her to do anything else.

Her mother had scheduled an appointment for her because Marisa seemed sad. Her parents had recently divorced, and that seemed to be the reason. Marisa refused to talk to me about the divorce. She was very direct. "I don't want to talk about it," she would say.

Before our final session, her mother asked if she could speak with me. I was apprehensive, because I did not think I was helping her daughter. I was being paid to play a game that, to tell the truth, I didn't even like.

Her mother took a seat and said, "I want to thank you so much for what you have done for Marisa. She is doing much better. You have done a great job with her. I don't know how you have done it, but she is totally different."

Needless to say, I felt a bit guilty, since I knew it was unlikely I had much to do with Marisa's improvement.

"I am really glad she is doing better," I replied. "Tell me, how does she seem better?"

"Well, every night I lie in bed with her and we talk," her mother said. "She has opened up so much since she started seeing you. We have finally been able to talk about the divorce. It has been really good for both of us."

It has been many years since I have done play therapy. Marisa and many other wonderful children and parents have taught me a great deal. One lesson I have learned is that psychologists often get more credit than they deserve. The real therapy almost always happens between parents and children.

My clinical practice is very different now. I have developed an approach, called Therapeutic Parenting, which you will learn about from reading this book. Using this approach, I spend most of my time helping parents solve problems with their own children. Instead of talking to a stranger in an office, these children get what they really need—a caring relationship with a mother or father who will listen and lovingly help them feel better about their worries and problems. Parents are much better therapists for their own children than I could ever be.

Talking Listening Connecting will teach you how to help your child. You can use this book in several ways. Part One, "Basic Skills of Therapeutic Parenting," tells you how to develop a warm and caring relationship with your child and how to use your values when solving problems. For some parents, using these fundamentals of parenting will be enough to resolve any problem that their child is experiencing. You may find all the answers you need for connecting with your child in the first six chapters.

Some parents, however, need more information about how to handle specific problems. Part Two, "Therapeutic Parenting in Action," helps you to solve these problems with your child. You may only need to read one of the chapters in the second half of the book to get the answers you need. For example, if your child has low self-esteem and you want to help him feel better about himself, you may only need to read Chapter 12, "Self-Esteem," for an explanation on why children develop low self-esteem and how you can help your child develop more confidence and become self-reliant.

You may also benefit from reading other chapters in Part Two, even if your child does not have those particular problems. Each chapter is filled with specific suggestions about how to talk to your child and how to develop solutions to problems. For example, even if your child is not depressed or does not have a problem with anger, you'll still find some useful tips that will enhance your relationship and refine your parenting skills.

The techniques that you will learn are the same ones that psychologists use in treating children. These techniques are easy to learn. Doing therapy with children is usually not that complicated. You don't need years of training to master these skills. Rather, you will see how to enhance what you do naturally—be caring and helpful to your child.

All the strategies you will learn are based on the philosophy that there is a solution to every problem. One of your jobs as a parent is to teach your child this lesson. You want your child to be an active problem solver who never gives up until she finds a solution to any problem. Children who are raised with this attitude are resilient and competent.

Many solutions to problems are remarkably simple and don't require complex psychological intervention. I have been taught this lesson by my clients. I remember seeing a nine-year-old boy who had become terrified after seeing one of the *Scream* movies. He was scared that someone was going to break into his house and kill him and his family. He was having great difficulty falling asleep. He was staying up very late, disrupting the whole house with his crying and desperate pleas for reassurance. He wanted to sleep with his parents every night.

I began working with this boy and his family using many of the strategies that you will learn in Chapter 10, "Anxious Children." In the first session, I told him about a few techniques that I thought would help him cope with his anxiety. I carefully explained the physiology of anxiety. He was very attentive, and I thought the session went quite well.

The next week when I asked him how his problem with sleeping was going, he told me it was completely resolved. He said he was sleeping the whole night, every night. I asked him what had led to this improvement. I was confident I would hear something like this: "Dr. Rosen, those ideas you gave me about how to handle my anxiety worked so well, that I am all better." But to my surprise, this is what he told me about why he was sleeping so well: "My mother had the idea that I should brush my teeth earlier in the evening. I had been waiting until I was tired before I brushed my teeth. After I finished brushing, I was all woken up and couldn't fall asleep. So my mother told me to brush my teeth before I get tired. Now when I'm sleepy, I can just lay in bed and fall asleep."

I certainly was pleased that he was doing so much better. "What about those ideas we talked about last week?" I asked, still hoping maybe I had something to do with the success.

"Could you tell me what you said again?" he replied. "I don't remember."

Simple solutions developed by parents with their children are always best. For those problems where you need additional assistance, this book offers strategies based on well-established principles of therapy. You will learn to trust your common sense, find solutions to problems, and strengthen the connection between you and your child.

Acknowledgments

Writing a book is not the same as publishing a book. To get a book published, an author needs to find people who believe in the merits of his work. I am lucky to have found talented people who were willing to take a chance and support an unknown author. I am thankful to my agent, Ed Knappman of New England Publishing Associates, for his professionalism and guidance. I am especially appreciative for the unwavering and enthusiastic support of Randy Ladenheim-Gil at Alpha Books.

Several people made important contributions to this book through conscientious editing and thoughtful commentary. Lynn Northrup, development editor, was helpful, hard-working, and always right on target with suggestions. I also want to thank Kathy Bidwell and the rest of the production staff at Alpha for their diligent assistance. I am particularly grateful to my colleague, Ellen Kay, Ed.D., for her astute clinical insights regarding case material, constructive feedback, and detailed editing of the manuscript.

I want to acknowledge the families with whom I have worked and whose stories appear in this book. These parents and children inspire me every day with their commitment to creating caring relationships and their willingness to find new ways to solve problems.

Since this is a book about parenting, it is, at many levels, a reflection of my family. I want to give special thanks to my wife, Karen, for teaching me so much about child development and for patiently supporting my writing. I also owe loving thanks to the people who taught me the most about parenting—my four terrific children. To my daughter Rachel, thanks for your careful reading of the manuscript and your help with the resources section. Joshua, thanks for helping prepare the manuscript and for your much-needed technical assistance. Emily, thank you for helping me understand the importance of protecting relationships. Finally, Seth, thanks for your creative and humorous suggestions for titles and for never letting me take myself too seriously.

Trademarks

All terms mentioned in this book that are known to be or are suspected of being trademarks or service marks have been appropriately capitalized. Alpha Books and Pearson Education, Inc., cannot attest to the accuracy of this information. Use of a term in this book should not be regarded as affecting the validity of any trademark or service mark.

Part One

Basic Skills of Therapeutic Parenting

Chapter 1

The New Challenges of Parenting

It is a daunting challenge to raise children in today's world. Life used to be simple for kids; they lived in a slow-paced world with consistent messages and traditional values. As a parent, you understand how things have changed. Your child is being bombarded by messages on television and radio that are not consistent with your values. He is immersed in a culture that glorifies sex and aggression, while pressuring him to be popular with peers, successful in school, and to excel at sports. These are formidable challenges for any child and his parents.

Given the current conditions, you cannot prevent your child from experiencing some degree of stress and conflict. This does not mean that it is impossible to raise happy and emotionally healthy children. Rather, you need to understand how your role as a parent has changed. It is no longer enough to be loving toward your child to ensure she will become a secure and responsible person. Certainly, all children need love. However, your child also needs to learn how to deal with the conflicting messages she receives outside of your family. She must internalize values that will assist her in making good choices. Your child also needs to develop the skills for coping with expanding expectations and increasing stress. Your child will need your help to find her way through this maze without getting lost.

Today's Children

Sadly, children are showing greater levels of emotional distress today than ever before. Many children are overly angry or depressed. Others have low self-esteem. Many children are defiant and oppositional to parents or teachers and do not complete their schoolwork or do their chores. Some children have perplexing behavior problems that do not seem to improve regardless of what their parents try to remedy the situation. Other children are well behaved, but anxious and fearful. Many children experience painful social situations, including being teased by peers or being excluded from games or social events. All of these children need help from their parents to overcome their problems and feel better about themselves.

You may be worried about your child. Perhaps he has been showing signs of distress, and his behavior has been difficult to manage. You worry about his future but are not sure you have the skills to deal with his issues. Since there is so much at stake, you feel a sense of urgency. If your attempts to reassure him have not succeeded, you may have even considered taking him to a child psychologist. You want to do what is best but are not sure if he needs therapy.

Choosing the right therapist for a child can be difficult. Ask your child's pediatrician for recommendations of therapists who specialize in working with children. If your friends have taken their children for therapy, ask them if they were satisfied with the treatment. Try to develop a list of three or more potential candidates, then call each therapist and interview them before scheduling an appointment for your child (see the list on page 6 for questions to ask). Therapists are accustomed to these phone calls. If a therapist you contact is not open to answering your questions, choose another person from your list. It's important that you feel comfortable with the person who will be helping your child.

Does Your Child Need Therapy?

Here are some guidelines to help you decide whether to get counseling for your child. Schedule an appointment with a child psychologist if your child exhibits any of the following behavior:

- ❖ Is threatening to hurt himself or others
- ❖ Is threatening suicide
- ❖ Has hurt herself on purpose (for example, has cut herself)
- ❖ Has been repeatedly aggressive
- ❖ Has been through a serious trauma, especially any kind of abuse
- ❖ Has had a major change in how she is acting or feeling for reasons you do not understand
- ❖ Says he is hearing voices or has very strange ideas
- ❖ Seems confused
- ❖ Has symptoms of an eating disorder such as stopping eating or making herself vomit
- ❖ Has severe mood swings
- ❖ Has compulsive behaviors or rituals that interfere with his functioning
- ❖ Is abusing drugs or alcohol
- ❖ Is engaging in high-risk behaviors

Questions to Ask a Psychologist About Counseling

If you have decided to take your child for therapy, here are some questions to ask the therapist during the initial phone call:

- ❖ "Do you specialize in working with children?"
- ❖ "What kind of therapy will you provide my child?"
- ❖ "Will you tell me what is happening in your sessions?"
- ❖ "Will I be included in your sessions?"
- ❖ "Will you consult with me about questions I have concerning my child's problems?"
- ❖ "How many sessions do you think it will take for the counseling to help my child?"
- ❖ "How will you know when it is time to stop counseling?"
- ❖ "How should I explain to my child what you do?"
- ❖ "What do you charge for treatment?"
- ❖ "Will my insurance cover your fees?"

Like most kids, your child may feel uncomfortable talking to a stranger and will give you a hard time if you force him to go. You do not want him to resent you or feel defective because you made him see a "shrink." As a devoted and loving parent, you do not want to overreact by taking him for treatment he may not need. You wonder if there is an alternative, another way to help without seeking professional intervention.

Fortunately, there is another option. You can learn how to help your child overcome his problems and develop healthy ways to cope with the typical issues all children face. This book will teach you the same techniques that therapists use in treating children. Once you learn these skills, you will be able to help your child develop more adaptive behavior, cope with stress, make more friends, and be more caring to siblings. You can teach your child to understand her own feelings and express her anger and frustrations more appropriately. Most importantly, you can instill values that will regulate her decisions and choices throughout her life.

The Parent As Therapist

Not only can you learn how therapists do this, you can do it better. Parents can be more effective than highly trained therapists in making meaningful changes in the lives of their children. As a parent, you are part of your child's real world. You are his primary role model. Your relationship is not restricted to a once-a-week hourly time slot where your child plays out situations in an office. You are in a powerful and influential position to help your child learn appropriate behavior. You can intervene at the best possible moment to help your child change and grow.

This book is about helping you raise an emotionally healthy child during these complicated times. You cannot be just a parent anymore; you are required to be both parent and therapist. You must continuously intervene to support and counsel your child, while simultaneously meeting your traditional parental responsibilities.

To help parents meet these challenges, I've developed a program which I call Therapeutic Parenting. I'll be referring to this unique approach throughout the book to show you how you can help your child learn to be a problem solver.

What Is Therapeutic Parenting?

Therapeutic Parenting is a relationship-based approach for you to help your child deal with problems and make good decisions. When children are stressed and have behavior problems, they are unhappy with themselves and frustrating to their parents. As these frustrations build without resolution, relationships between parents and children deteriorate. Many loving parents begin to yell at their children or punish them in an attempt to correct their children's misbehavior. When these strategies do not work, the relationship is damaged, and parents and children feel estranged and unhappy. Most parents feel a sense of loss and disappointment. Parenting is supposed to be fulfilling and enjoyable. The most important goal of Therapeutic Parenting is to ensure that you have a warm and caring relationship with your child regardless of the problems or challenges you encounter.

Therapeutic Parenting also emphasizes the importance of instilling values. Teaching values is at the heart of raising children, and you will learn techniques that will greatly assist you in this goal. You will also learn how to help your child feel more comfortable talking to you about his feelings, problems, and conflicts. From these discussions with your child, you will be able to help him change the way he thinks and acts. You will also help him to find new solutions to problems. Therapeutic Parenting will ensure that you have a strong, loving relationship with your child that will allow you to communicate and solve problems together.

If your child needs help in dealing with emotional, behavioral, or moral issues, it does not mean you are a bad or inadequate parent. Many wonderful parents have children with behavior problems or children who are overwhelmed by intense feelings. Even excellent parents with great kids need help in dealing with these complicated situations. Therapeutic Parenting will prepare you to meet this challenge and ensure your child's success.

Throughout this book I've included case examples of families I have seen in my practice who have learned to use Therapeutic Parenting. Names and other identifying information have been changed in order to protect the confidentiality of the families.

Part One, "Basic Skills of Therapeutic Parenting," focuses on the basic skills of Therapeutic Parenting, including how to create and maintain a caring relationship, teach values, and set effective limits. These parenting fundamentals create the necessary foundation for helping your child learn to cope with problems. You will also learn TLC (Talking, Listening, and Connecting), which is a simple but powerful format for discussing problems. Part One is an overview of parenting and problem solving that provides a model for raising happy, well-adjusted children.

Part Two, "Therapeutic Parenting in Action," addresses how to apply the principles and techniques of Therapeutic Parenting to specific problems, such as conflict between siblings, excessive worrying, and teasing by peers. The skills you will learn can be applied to children of all ages and both sexes. Of course, there are some problems that do require professional intervention. Some children have complicated issues that require sophisticated treatment. Professional help is particularly important if your child is in danger of hurting herself or others or is showing signs of serious emotional problems. This book will clarify what signs to look for so you will know if you need to seek professional counseling.

Even well-adjusted children benefit when parents have a wide repertoire of skills for handling emotional and behavioral issues. As you know, children do not come with operating manuals. Parenting is challenging and confusing. This book will teach you how to handle those situations that worry all parents. Don't take it personally if your child needs this help or if you are not sure what to do. It does not mean there is something wrong with him or that you are not a good parent. You can learn these skills and help your child overcome his problems.

9

Once you understand how to intervene on your child's behalf, you will feel better about yourself as a parent. You will have more self-confidence and project a more secure image. You will have an even stronger relationship with your child as you teach her to embrace and follow your values. Nothing matters more than your child's happiness and success. Help her to negotiate her life course by modeling and teaching her the skills that make this possible.

Key Points to Remember

❖ Many children are stressed and confused.

❖ As a parent, you are in the best position to help your child.

❖ Teaching values is crucial to effective parenting.

❖ Therapeutic Parenting will help you raise a happy, well-adjusted child.

Chapter 2

Creating a Caring Relationship

As Martha walked up the stairs toward her son's bedroom, she was fuming. She had already asked five times for her nine-year-old son, Vinny, to clean his room. He had left his clothes on the bedroom floor. His schoolbooks were scattered across his desk and bureau. There were miscellaneous papers and toys littered everywhere. She had tried to be patient with him, but her frustration rose with each ignored request. Now, as she approached his bedroom, she could hear the sounds of a video game. She knew he had ignored her request once again and, instead, was playing.

"That's it! I've had it with you," Martha screamed as she stomped into the room. "Turn off that game right now!"

Vinny looked startled. He reached to turn off the video game. Martha was not finished. "I am sick and tired of you ignoring me. You are a spoiled brat. I give you everything you want. Here you are playing a video game that I bought for you. But when I ask you to clean up this pigpen, you won't do it. You are an ungrateful, selfish brat. I am sick of this. Get this room cleaned now. Do you hear me?"

Vinny did not say a word. He began to scramble around the room and pick up his mess. He began to cry as he put his dirty clothes in the hamper. Martha stood with her hands on her hips watching to make sure that Vinny really did his chore. However, she did not feel any satisfaction or relief that her son was finally cleaning his room. She wondered why the only time he responded to her requests was when she yelled.

Martha walked back down the stairs. She was no longer angry, but she was sad. Vinny was a good boy, and she loved him dearly. She hated yelling and hated how she felt about herself for screaming like a lunatic. She did not respect herself when she got this angry. Martha felt trapped. How could she help him to develop good habits without having to scream? She was not sure she knew how to do this, but she did not feel good about what she had just done. She decided to walk back upstairs and help Vinny clean his room.

Martha's frustration was understandable. Vinny was not meeting his responsibilities. However, her attempts to hold him accountable were damaging their relationship. This chapter will help you to remain focused on the key goal of parenting: developing and maintaining a warm and caring relationship with your child. This is the first step in Therapeutic Parenting and the single most important goal in raising children.

Building on a Solid Foundation

A caring relationship is the foundation for everything you hope to accomplish as a parent. Without a warm relationship, your child will be insecure, unhappy, and uncooperative. If your child feels estranged from you, he will not do what you ask and will angrily reject your beliefs. On the other hand, if your child feels nurtured and cared for, he will respond to your guidance and adopt the values you teach.

Therapeutic Parenting is a model for how to raise a child who is emotionally secure, able to solve problems, and guided by a strong commitment to values. These goals are possible only if you succeed in preserving a loving relationship. The techniques that you will learn for helping your child deal with problems are based on the assumption that you have a close and warm connection. These skills require that you and your child communicate and solve problems together. If your relationship is damaged and your child is uncomfortable sharing her feelings, you will not be able to help her.

Maintaining a consistently caring relationship is the greatest challenge of parenting. Loving a child is not the same as having a warm and caring relationship with a child. All parents love their children. Of course, all parents also get annoyed and angry. This is appropriate and necessary, at times. The problem is that some parents and children have so many frustrating interactions that the relationship is damaged. Many parents yell and punish their children in an attempt to correct misbehavior and teach responsibility. The result of these discipline techniques is that parents and children grow distant. Once the relationship has been damaged, it can take a long time to heal.

You may find it difficult to be warm toward your child, even though you truly love him. While you want to be sensitive and kind, his behavior and your lifestyle can get in the way. It is difficult to be caring when your child is whining, noncompliant, or purposely provoking you. After a long day, all parents struggle to find patience in dealing with annoying behavior. When kids misbehave, warmth dissolves into conflict.

Some parents struggle to be nurturing because their own parents were not affectionate with them while they were growing up. Parenting styles are often passed down through generations. If your parents were not warm toward you, it will be more difficult to create this kind of relationship with your child. However, you *can* break this pattern and prepare your child to be a better parent by creating a loving relationship with him now. When your child has children of his own, he will be naturally affectionate and loving toward them.

If you feel estranged from your child or your relationship is not as warm as you would like it to be, don't despair. There is a lot you can do to fix this problem. Therapeutic Parenting will show you how to teach your child to be responsible, while creating the closeness your child needs.

Effective Communication

Of course, maintaining a warm relationship does not mean that you or your child can never get angry. When expressed appropriately, your anger can be a helpful message about how your child's actions affect others. Your role includes setting limits on her behavior, and this may make her angry. However, you must always prioritize your relationship over every other issue. When you get angry or need to set limits, do it in a way that protects the relationship and models how you want your child to express herself.

Here are some guidelines for how to create and maintain a warm and caring relationship with your child:

- ❖ Try not to yell.
- ❖ Set limits in a calm tone.
- ❖ Do not say mean things or criticize your child.
- ❖ Make punishments fair. Punish misbehavior with the smallest consequence that still reinforces your message.
- ❖ Negotiate limits; things do not always have to go your way.
- ❖ Be positive and appreciative. Use praise as much as possible.
- ❖ Be affectionate.
- ❖ Follow through on your promises.
- ❖ Model the behavior you want your child to learn.
- ❖ Make time for the relationship. Do not fit your child in around your schedule.

❖ Accept your child for who he is, and do not try to change him into someone he is not.

❖ Be clear about what you expect and consistent in how you respond.

❖ Be consistent in your demeanor. Do not turn warmth on and off.

To help your child deal with her issues, she must believe she can talk to you about whatever is bothering her. She needs to trust you and not worry that she will regret sharing her feelings. If she sees you as empathic and accepting of her perspective, she will want to talk to you. When she needs advice, she will want your guidance. When she needs support and comfort, she will receive the greatest solace from you. These interactions are at the heart of parenting and are essential for helping a child who is sad, afraid, unsure, or distraught.

Open communication is critical, since it will enable you to help your child learn to solve problems. He will tell you if he is sad or nervous. He will talk to you about his problems with his peers or siblings. He will also be open to discussing his own misbehavior and will listen to your feedback. There may even be times when he will tell you what you are doing that is upsetting him. Trust is imperative to this process. Your child must be certain that no matter what he tells you he can count on an empathic response.

As your child begins to tell you how she feels and what is bothering her, you must be acutely aware of how you respond. Most of the time you will find it easy to be empathic and reassuring when your child expresses herself. However, some of what you may hear will be upsetting. You may disagree with your child's goals and be disappointed in her lack of motivation to solve problems. You may disagree with your child's perspective on a situation. You may feel defensive if your child sees you critically. The way you respond to your child's criticism, complaints, and opinions is extremely important. Your goal is to support honest dialogue. Your response will determine whether she will continue to share her feelings.

How to Be a Good Listener

Psychologists use several simple techniques for making their clients feel comfortable when talking. Try these strategies when you talk to your child:

❖ Make eye contact with your child but don't stare.

❖ Smile a lot while you are listening.

❖ Nod your head to show you understand what she is saying.

❖ Label his feelings for him. For example, say, "You must have been pretty mad when that happened."

❖ Summarize what your child has said to you.

❖ Never make your child regret that she has shared her feelings or opinions by being critical or harsh.

Let's say your child has been disrespectful, and you have a conversation with him about this problem. Your child tells you that he thinks you have been disrespectful to him. He says that you say mean things and that he is only reacting to your disrespect. Let's assume that you do not agree with your child's perspective. You do not like what you hear, both because it is inaccurate, and it seems your child is not accepting responsibility for his own behavior. You decide to give your child this feedback and to express your anger over his accusation. You tell him you do not like what he is saying and that you disagree with him. You tell him why he is wrong and how he should act differently. You tell him it makes you angry when he criticizes you to deflect responsibility from himself.

Even if all of this feedback were accurate, your child will not want to talk to you again. Instead of feeling understood, he will feel criticized and blamed. He will feel vulnerable after having shared his concerns and perceptions. He will regret he told you how he felt. He will not entrust you with his feelings again.

You must respond with compassion and empathy during these conversations. Even if you disagree or are offended by his opinion, try to react with sensitivity and without being defensive. This is a difficult style to master. The critical issue is recognizing that maintaining open lines of communication is more important than any topic or disagreement. As you look for the best way to react, remain focused on your goal: Protecting a relationship that allows for communication and problem solving.

Here are some suggestions for what you can say to encourage further sharing:

"I'm glad you told me how you feel."

"I want to understand your point of view. I may not agree with how you see things, but your perspective matters to me."

"Some of what you're saying is upsetting, but I want to know your honest opinion. It's important that you tell me your true feelings."

"If I'm doing things that are bothering you, I want to know. I won't get mad at you for telling me these things. I can't promise I'll change what I'm doing, but I will listen carefully and see if there's another way for me to handle the situation."

These statements are accepting of your child's perspective and facilitate honest communication. You do not need to agree with everything your child says or accept full responsibility for issues she may have with you. Rather, you promise to try and understand her point of view and be open to new ways to address issues. You also model how you want her to respond to your feedback. These responses prevent further damage to the relationship by avoiding defensive or critical comments. In future chapters, you will learn more about what to say to your child as she expresses feelings or discusses problems.

Here is a case example of a mother who changed her approach in order to develop a warmer relationship with her daughter.

Elaine was a working mother who had two children. Her daughter, Alexis, was 10, and her son, James, 4. Her husband, Don, worked long hours and traveled frequently on business.

Elaine loved being a mother and enjoyed her time with her children. However, her relationship with Alexis was strained. Alexis was strong-willed and defiant. She gave Elaine a hard time getting ready for school in the morning and was often late for the school bus. Elaine was frazzled in the mornings trying to get James ready and to get herself to work on time. She was frustrated when Alexis was uncooperative. She yelled in order to get Alexis to finish her morning routine.

Alexis gradually become more defiant. She talked back to her mother, refused to do chores, and often had an angry demeanor. As Alexis's attitude worsened, the level of conflict between her and her mother increased. They fought often, especially when Elaine tried to get Alexis to meet her responsibilities. Things got bad enough that Elaine was considering taking Alexis to a therapist to see what was wrong. Elaine hoped a therapist could get her to talk about what was bothering her. She was worried that Alexis was harboring deep-seated anger and resentment. Elaine tried to get Alexis to discuss her feelings, but her daughter refused to talk to her.

Elaine came to see me for a consultation and to discuss the possibility of bringing Alexis for therapy. After seeing Alexis two times, I suggested that Elaine try to work through these issues with her daughter rather than bringing her to see me. I explained how much better it would be if Alexis could talk to her mother about what was bothering her. Elaine said that was what she wanted but did not know how to proceed.

The first step in this process was to reinstate the warmth that had dissipated. Elaine had been feeling guilty that she was yelling too much and not spending enough time with Alexis. Even when not yelling, she thought her tone was not as soft and friendly as it should be. Elaine also felt that she was too quick to punish Alexis for misbehavior. When she tried to get Alexis to talk about her feelings, Alexis was sullen and uncooperative. Alexis gave curt or sarcastic responses such as, "What do you care?"

Elaine embarked on a campaign to change the way she interacted with Alexis. She committed herself to controlling the yelling and to using a friendly tone whenever they interacted. She was more affectionate. She began to model the kind of communication she hoped to teach Alexis and share her feelings in a way that did not blame her daughter. When Alexis was uncooperative or needed limits, Elaine responded firmly, yet calmly.

After a month of diligently working on their relationship, Elaine began to notice differences. Alexis was less hostile and warmer in her interactions with her mother. She was more agreeable in the mornings while getting ready for school. Alexis also became more open to talking. Elaine told her that she wanted to understand what Alexis was feeling. Alexis started to open up and said she felt neglected by her mother. She felt her mother had time for her job and her brother, but not for her. She felt her mother was always angry and did not want to spend time with her.

Once Alexis began to express herself, Elaine felt it was a very important step. Elaine apologized for her role in the relationship becoming distant and pledged to continue to be more available. She told Alexis how proud she was of her for being able to express her feelings. She also told Alexis how special it was to feel close, once again, with her daughter. They agreed to continue talking and working on their relationship.

The key to getting Alexis to talk about how she felt was to change the nature of her relationship with her mother. Once this was accomplished, Alexis felt safe and ready to trust her mother with her feelings.

All parents want to have positive interactions with their children. All parents have days when they lose their patience and are short-tempered. When this happens to you, return to being warm and caring as quickly as possible. Your relationship with your child is resilient. It will bounce back from difficult times. Don't worry or feel guilty when you have a bad day. Commit yourself to developing a healthy and close relationship. Don't give up until you get it right.

Key Points to Remember

❖ A warm, caring relationship is the most important goal of parenting.

❖ A warm relationship is the first step in helping your child solve problems.

❖ Learn to set limits and express your frustration in ways that do not damage your relationship with your child.

❖ Respond with sensitivity and empathy when your child tells you how he feels.

Chapter 3

It's All About Values

"*Mom, Cindy's on the phone,*" *yelled 11-year-old Melissa. Cindy was her mother's best friend. Cindy and her mother talked on the phone every afternoon. Melissa loved to sit and listen. Of course, she could only hear one side of the conversation.*

"*You're kidding,*" *her mother said to Cindy. "How much weight did she gain? ... No way. She was always so thin. I haven't seen her in five years. I would have loved to have seen her.*"

Melissa tried to figure out who her mother and Cindy were describing. Her mother was laughing. "She was always a little too loose anyway. I bet she must have looked pretty silly wearing such tight pants. What did you say?"

More laughing. "I can't believe you said that. If you ever said that to me, I'd smack you. Are you going to tell Evelyn? Yeah, I think you should. Evelyn never forgave her for trying to steal Dave away from her. Evelyn would love to hear how fat she is. Definitely ... yeah, tell her. Okay, call me later and tell me what she says. Okay, bye."

Her mother hung up the phone, a smile still on her face. "Mom, who were you talking about?" Melissa asked.

"Oh, just someone Cindy and I knew from high school. You don't know her."

"Do you know who is really getting fat, Mom?" Melissa asked. "Greta. She is so fat. She was wearing this sweater today that looked so stupid."

"Sweetheart," her mother said. "That's not nice. I don't want you talking that way about Greta. She is your friend."

Children, like Melissa, watch and listen to their parents. Most of what children learn from their parents comes through observation. Children act like their parents and believe in the same things. Modeling is the best way to teach children good habits and strong values. Unfortunately, many parents inadvertently confuse their children by believing one way and acting another. Certainly, Melissa learned a different lesson than her mother intended to teach.

The Importance of Values

A core component of Therapeutic Parenting is teaching values. Children need values so they can develop self-control and make ethical decisions. When children are young, they are not cognitively capable of understanding and following a set of beliefs. Rather, they depend on their parents for guidance and regulation. As they get older, children must learn to function on their own so that parents do not always have to tell them how to behave. To successfully meet life's challenges, children must develop an internal guidance system to help them make good decisions. They need to know right from wrong. They must learn to accept responsibility and have the self-discipline to attain their goals.

It is your job to make sure that your child learns the values that will enable him to be a responsible and successful adult. Without this solid foundation, your child will struggle. He will be confused and inconsistent in his choices. He will act impulsively without regard for the effects of his actions on himself or others. For these reasons, he needs to have a set of rules to govern his behavior.

Values are like a blueprint that outlines the structure of a building. Your child must have a detailed picture of who she is and what she believes. She must be able to consult this blueprint when you are not available so she can know what to do. She must also have a way to evaluate herself. Her values provide a standard against which she can compare her behavior. When she is small, you can tell her you are proud of her or disappointed when she makes a wrong choice. When she is older, she will have to evaluate herself to decide if she has acted wisely and appropriately. To make these self-appraisals, she has to compare her actions to her value system. She needs to determine if her actions are consistent with the standards she has been raised to follow. When she has successfully acted in accordance with her beliefs, she will be proud of her accomplishments. When she violates her own value system, she will know she has made a mistake and be able to take corrective action.

The stronger the value system, the more effective your child will be in handling all situations. On the other hand, if he is unsure of what he believes, he will struggle to find direction and get into trouble. He will be easily influenced by others, strongly affected by peer pressure, and swayed by fads. He will be a follower, not a leader.

Clarify Your Values

The first step in teaching your child values is to make sure you know which values you want your child to learn. Some parents have a clear awareness of their values and can easily articulate them. Other parents, however, are confused about their values and have difficulty knowing what to teach. The lack of clearly defined values is a significant problem that requires correction.

How Clear Are Your Values?

Consider the following questions to get an idea of how clear your values are to you and your kids:

* What values do you remember being taught by your parents?

* Do you share the same values that your parents taught you?

* How have your values changed since you became a parent?

* What values have you actually discussed with your children?

* What values have not been discussed that should be?

* How have you taught values by how you act?

* In what ways is your behavior inconsistent with your values?

* Could your child tell you what values he has learned from you?

You do not have to identify every value that you want to teach. However, it is crucial to have several core values that are central to your parenting. For example, you may particularly value being kind and caring to others, including siblings. You may value acting responsibly and completing tasks. You might prioritize education, respectful behavior, politeness, cleanliness, or honesty. Think about which things you most want to teach your children. Then, give them the necessary feedback when their behavior does not conform to these values.

In addition, you must live your life according to your values. Remember that modeling is an extremely important method for teaching right from wrong. Your child learns a great deal from seeing how you act and how you solve problems. Make sure your actions are consistent with the values you teach. If you preach honesty but your child witnesses you being dishonest, she will be confused. Your credibility will be weakened, and she will not follow your advice.

Conduct an honest self-appraisal of how you act in front of your child. Be a good role model, especially when you talk to him. For example, you may tell him that you want him to be respectful. However, do you talk to him respectfully? Do you use swearwords but expect him not to swear? Do you yell when you are mad but get angry when he loses his temper? Do you criticize him for his faults but resent it when he criticizes you? Monitor your actions to ensure you are modeling your values. Children mirror the actions of their parents. If you see something in your child that you do not like, make sure he did not learn it from you.

Do Your Child's Interests Reflect Your Values?

Think about the interests, activities, and role models that your child enjoys. Which of them reflect your values?

- ❖ The television shows he watches
- ❖ The music she listens to
- ❖ The posters on his walls
- ❖ The movies she is allowed to watch
- ❖ The sports teams he plays for or watches on television
- ❖ Extracurricular activities she enjoys
- ❖ His favorite teachers
- ❖ Her favorite actors
- ❖ His favorite sports figures
- ❖ Her best friends

Use Values When Solving Problems

When your child has a problem or conflict, it is your job to make sure she uses values as part of the solution. It is not enough to comfort your child, nor is it sufficient to teach her a skill to cope with a problem. Your child must understand why you want her to act a certain way. Values explain why she should choose one path over another. Whenever you talk to your child about mistakes she has made, conflicts she has, or trouble she is in, you must make it clear what you believe is the right way to act and why. Teach her to use her beliefs as a way to regulate her behavior.

Without teaching your child these things, he may make his choices based on other factors, such as whether he gets in trouble. Or, he may act based on what gives him the most pleasure. While punishments and rewards are part of life and regulate a lot of what we do, they are not values. Your child needs to do what is right even if he does not get rewarded; and, he needs to act responsibly even if he thinks he can get away with improper behavior.

Therapeutic Parenting stresses finding solutions to problems that are grounded in values. For example, let's say your daughter is having a problem in school with her teacher. The teacher is giving her a hard time because he thinks your daughter has been clowning around in class and not doing her work. Your daughter tells you that she thinks the teacher is picking on her, is boring, and isn't teaching anything worthwhile. She admits that she talks back to her teacher because he is rude to her.

What would you say to your daughter in this situation? While you want to ensure your child is treated fairly, you also want to teach her to be respectful to teachers.

If you let your values guide you and communicate them to your daughter, the range of solutions becomes clear. First, you model respect for the teacher. If you say that the teacher is a loser and he should be fired, you will model disrespect. It would be hollow advice to tell your child to be respectful to a teacher for whom you have just shown disdain. Instead, you might say something like this:

> "I'm glad you came to me to talk about this. I'm proud of you for being honest, including the fact that you're honest about talking back to your teacher. We need to figure out what we're going to do. I will help you, and I will go into school, if necessary, to talk to your teacher. But whatever we decide to do, I expect you to be respectful. I know that you think he is boring, and I don't approve of him picking on you. I'll help you with that. However, I don't want you to talk back to him in a disrespectful manner. I do think you should tell him how you feel, but not in a way that's inappropriate. Let's talk about how you can do that and how I can help."

In this conversation, your child is given support for what she is going through in school. Her feelings and perspective are acknowledged and validated. There are also clear messages about values. You have told her you value that she has come to you about an issue and that she is being honest. You have also told her you expect her to be respectful and that this is an absolute requirement for any solution.

Caught Between Competing Values

A trouble spot for some parents occurs when they lose sight of one value while trying to teach another value. This problem led to difficulties for the parent in the following case example.

Bernie was a conscientious parent who wanted to make sure that his 12-year-old son, Adam, was successful in school. Bernie knew that Adam was bright and capable of doing well academically. However, he felt his son was an underachiever. He thought Adam was not trying hard enough to get good grades. He believed that Adam rushed through his homework and did not study as long as necessary. Adam was getting Bs, and he told his father he was satisfied with these grades.

Bernie was frustrated with Adam's low standards. He began to closely monitor how much time Adam spent on homework. Bernie insisted the work be done neatly and required Adam to do the work over if it was not up to his standards. They began to have daily arguments about homework. The process became time consuming, often taking two to three hours each night. Bernie felt his entire evening was used up being a homework monitor. He did not let his son talk on the phone, use the computer, or watch television until the work was done. Most nights, Adam went to bed as soon as the assignments were completed, because he did not finish until his bedtime.

Their relationship became strained and unpleasant. They both dreaded the nightly ritual of battling over homework. Adam became sullen and uncommunicative. He avoided his dad as much as possible. He started to refuse to do his chores or keep his room neat. He said he did not have time to do these tasks because his homework was taking so long to complete. Bernie started to punish Adam, taking away various privileges due to his lack of cooperation and overall bad attitude.

Adam brought home his next report card and Bernie was shocked. Adam's grades had dropped to all Cs and one D. Bernie was flabbergasted that his son's grades had gone down after all the effort he had put into helping him. He had hoped, that despite the conflict, Adam would benefit academically. Confused and disappointed, Bernie called me to make an appointment for a consultation.

During our first meeting, I asked Bernie about his values. He spoke of how important it was to raise a son who was responsible and capable. I asked him how much he valued having a close relationship with his son. He said it mattered a great deal. He felt bad that he and his son had not been getting along, but he believed it was his responsibility to ensure that his son learned to work hard and meet his potential. Bernie felt caught between competing values—his wish to have his son learn responsibility and his desire to have a warm relationship with him.

As he analyzed this dilemma, he realized that his way of prioritizing his values was not working. He now had a hostile relationship with Adam, and his son's grades had deteriorated as well. Bernie was not succeeding at either goal. By stressing grades and responsibility to such an extreme, he had damaged his relationship with his son to the point where Adam was rejecting his father's attempts to teach him an important lesson.

Bernie began to understand that to teach Adam his values, he first had to have a strong relationship with him. The only acceptable solution was one where Bernie could teach both values: the importance of hard work and the necessity of having a mutually caring and respectful relationship.

Bernie changed his approach. He carefully explained his values to his son. He said he felt he had made a mistake in pushing Adam so hard that they could not feel good about their relationship. He promised to do things differently and be more sensitive to Adam's feelings and needs. However, he also said he still wanted Adam to apply himself diligently to his schoolwork. He told his son he wanted to develop an agreement so that they would not battle over schoolwork while still ensuring that Adam worked conscientiously. They began a process of negotiation. Adam said he did not want his father hovering over him all night or nagging him to do his work. Adam agreed that he would not watch television or use the computer until all of his homework was completed. He said he wanted to be able to talk on the telephone with his friends when they called. He agreed that he would keep these conversations brief. Bernie and Adam both felt this was an acceptable arrangement, and they gave it a try. Their relationship quickly improved, as did Adam's grades.

Bernie was a caring and concerned parent. However, his anxiety about his son's future caused him to focus too intently on one aspect of his values. Once he examined his values and what he wanted to accomplish, he realized he needed to make a correction. He showed his son that he valued their relationship and admitted he had made a mistake. He told Adam what he believed and then backed it up by acting accordingly.

Therapeutic Parenting emphasizes your relationship with your child and the teaching of values. The next chapter will explain more about how to use values while solving problems. Using these skills will enhance your relationship with your child, make you feel more competent as a parent, and give your child the moral building blocks for guiding his decisions throughout his life.

Key Points to Remember

❖ Teach your child your values.

❖ Model your values for your child.

❖ Maintain a caring relationship while teaching values.

❖ Remind your child of what you expect of him when dealing with problems or conflicts.

Chapter 4

The Four Rules for Setting Limits

"You're grounded."

"Oh, come on, Dad," complained 13-year-old Amy. "I'll rake the leaves now."

"That's right. You will rake the leaves now," her father, Peter, replied with an icy edge to his voice. "But you are still grounded for a week."

"A week! Dad, that's not fair. I just got off grounding three days ago."

"Well, I guess it's time you learned your lesson then, isn't it? You screwed up twice this time. First, you didn't rake the leaves. Second, when I called today to ask if you had finished raking, you said you were all done. That was a lie."

"Dad, I was going to do it. I thought I was going to finish before you got home," Amy pleaded. "You ended up coming home early. I would have finished if you came home at your regular time."

"You lied to me," Peter was almost yelling. "You need to be more responsible. I am sick and tired of you shirking your responsibilities. Think about that while you're grounded."

"Please, Dad. There's a dance at school tomorrow night."

"You know the rules. Next time, do your job and stop this lying," Peter said firmly.

"Screw you!" Amy screamed as she turned to walk away. "Rake your own god-damned leaves!"

"Watch your mouth, young lady. And you get over here and start raking."

"Go to hell. That's where I am living with you. I spend my whole life being grounded. I never can do anything fun. Either I have to do chores, or I'm grounded!" Amy was red-faced from screaming. She ran toward her bedroom.

"Amy, you get back here ... Amy? Okay, you just earned another week of grounding. And you will still rake those leaves. Do you hear me?"

There was no response to Peter's question.

By now you recognize the importance of prioritizing your relationship with your child. Adhering to this principle will be most difficult when your child misbehaves, is irresponsible, or violates your values. This was the dilemma that Peter faced with Amy. Like all parents, Peter didn't want to punish his daughter. However, he felt he had to do something to teach her a lesson.

Your job includes setting limits when your child does something wrong. Learning to set limits while protecting your relationship and teaching values is a real juggling act. In this chapter, you will learn how to simultaneously do these three key components of Therapeutic Parenting.

When to Set Limits

Setting limits refers to the response you give your child when she does not follow rules or meet her responsibilities. Your limits must be fair, consistent, and age-appropriate. Limit setting is tricky. When used effectively, limits will help your child learn values and behave appropriately. When used improperly, limits will intensify your child's misbehavior. If your limits are harsh, your child will be angry and will retaliate with stubbornness and oppositional behavior. If your limits are inconsistent, your child will be confused and will not learn the lessons you are trying to teach.

Your child needs to get clear feedback about what you expect, including how to behave and what will happen if he does not comply. You have to be consistent with these expectations so that you can communicate them to your child and give accurate feedback. When your child meets these expectations, make sure you let him know he has been successful and that you are pleased. When your child does not meet these expectations, you should set a limit.

Unfortunately, when your child misbehaves, you are most likely to be upset. When you are angry or frustrated, you are most at-risk to overreact. If you set limits based on emotion alone, you may be too harsh or insensitive. It is during these moments that your relationship is most in jeopardy. Here are four rules to follow to help you set effective limits.

Rule #1: Impose

Limits should always be as mild as possible while still helping your child learn from her mistakes. Consequences should be appropriate to the child's age and relevant to the offense. In other words, the punishment should fit the crime. Punishments that are harsh have a negative impact on children. Instead of teaching a helpful lesson, harsh punishments make children feel that their parents are unfair. This happens when parents make punishments too long, for example by "grounding" a child for a week or taking television away for a month. Long punishments make children feel hopeless about ever behaving well enough to earn back their privileges.

Choosing a limit that is effective and developmentally appropriate can be challenging. Here is a list of consequences that you can try when setting limits for younger children (ages 4 to 8):

- ❖ Ignore your child until his behavior conforms to expectations. Let your child know you are not going to be paying attention to him until he does what is expected.

- ❖ Take away a toy your child is using or activity she is playing while she is misbehaving. This may mean taking away a toy a child has thrown or stopping a child from playing a game when she has just hit a playmate.

- ❖ Tell your child he cannot do a fun activity, such as watching television, until he has met your expectation or stopped misbehaving.

Many parents use time-out as a consequence for misbehavior. If you choose to use time-out, keep the length of the time out as short as possible. Do not overuse time-out, or your child will feel she is in jail. Do not use time-out if you have to physically drag your child, or if you have to physically force her to stay. As an alternative to time-out, you can ignore your child or you can leave the room until she meets your expectations. This technique can accomplish the same results as time-out without the power struggles.

For pre-teen and early teenage children (ages 9 to 14), there are additional consequences that can be imposed. Since these children are older, they can make better connections between their behavior and the consequences. Here are some limits you can set for this age group:

- ❖ Restrict access to fun activities for a period of time. For example, when a child has been aggressive, make a family rule of no television or computer for two hours.

- ❖ Assign extra chores to compensate for destruction of property.

* Don't give rides to friends' houses or to the mall after a child has been disrespectful or refused to meet household or school responsibilities.

* Withhold allowance for not meeting expectations.

* Don't provide special treats or buy special items if the child refuses to cooperate with you or is verbally abusive.

Rule #2: Model How to Handle Frustration and Anger

Your demeanor and tone are very important when setting limits, perhaps even more important than the limit itself. A harsh tone and hurtful criticism severely injure a relationship. Anytime you are frustrated or angry with your child, you have an opportunity to teach him a lesson about how to handle his own feelings. He will learn by observing you. Do you scream? Do you make comments that you really do not mean? Do you throw things or bang around the house? Do you spank your child or use physical intimidation to force compliance or punish misbehavior? The worst damage from spanking is not the physical pain. Rather, it is the emotional harm inflicted on your relationship. If you do any of these things, expect your child to use the same techniques when he is upset.

If your anger rages, you will have a difficult time convincing your child to trust you. When you set limits, speak in a calm voice. Don't debate your limits. Explain your rationale, but do not get dragged into a prolonged dialogue. It's okay to express how you feel. Tell your child that you are angry, frustrated, or disappointed. However, avoid yelling or harsh comments as a way to communicate these feelings.

Harsh Comments Can Last a Lifetime

Everyone knows that harsh comments can be hurtful. Try the following exercise for yourself. You may be surprised at how well you remember.

❖ Recall or write down the worst things a person has ever said about you.

❖ Identify the relationship you had with this person.

❖ Estimate out how long this conversation lasted.

❖ Calculate how many months or years it has been since this happened.

Here are some things for you to notice from this exercise:

❖ People vividly remember harsh comments long after they were made.

❖ People still feel hurt about these remarks years later.

❖ The person making the hurtful comments was usually someone important—a parent, teacher, or close friend.

❖ The length of the conversation or remark that caused this lasting pain was usually less than a minute.

Rule #3: Set Fewer Limits on Teenagers

As your child gets older, your limit setting and structuring of her routine need to change. The older your child, the less you need to rely on consequences to teach right from wrong. Consequences imposed from limit setting often have a negative effect on teenagers. Younger children need structure and limits. On the other hand, teens rebel against rules, structure, and' consequences. Overusing these strategies with teens will lead to defiance. They will intentionally engage in behavior that violates your values and retaliate against control imposed upon them. These power struggles ensue because teens are developing their own identities and establishing their independence.

Let's examine a common battleground between parents and children to see how limit setting should change as children get older. A typical problem is how to respond to a child with a messy bedroom. You should handle this situation differently depending on the age of your child. With a younger child, your job is to teach him age-appropriate responsibility. This includes providing a structure to follow and limits when he deviates from acceptable behavior. For example, you may tell him that he cannot do fun activities until he cleans his room.

On the other hand, if your 16-year-old daughter has a messy room, you should be careful about setting limits. If you start lecturing and then grounding her, your relationship will suffer. Most likely her room will not get cleaned, either. This is a place to avoid a battle and not use punishment. However, it is important to say, "I am upset about how you keep your room. It bothers me that you live like this and don't take better care of your things and our home. It also hurts me, because I feel that my wishes are being ignored." This feedback about the behavior labels the values of acting responsibly and being sensitive to the needs of others. After this conversation, you should insist she keep the door to her room closed, thereby avoiding additional power struggles. (And since most teens cherish their privacy, chances are you won't have to insist they keep their door closed!)

Setting fewer limits on teens does not mean that you ignore or condone misbehavior. It will always be part of your role to discuss problems with your child, regardless of his age. Therapeutic Parenting is a model for how to engage in this reciprocal dialogue. However, punishing teenagers decreases communication. Your child will learn more from talking to you about his decisions than he will from punishment.

37

Rule #4: Emphasize Values When Setting Limits

As discussed in Chapter 3, "It's All About Values," you should always discuss your values as part of limit setting. Your child should know why you have set a limit. When she makes a mistake, it is a critical time to teach values. Explain your priorities and discuss what you believe is the right way to act. Remember that it will take time for young children to internalize these beliefs.

The process of integrating values and limits is more complicated with a teenager. Your job is to make sure your teenager holds himself accountable to *his* values. He does not need limits to understand right from wrong. He knows what is expected and can evaluate his actions to see if he has acted responsibly. Knowing what is right, however, does not mean he will always do the right thing. With your teen, you should engage in dialogue about his beliefs and challenge him to look at his actions. Ask him if he is happy with his choices. This dialogue is important for helping your child refine his value system. In this way, you are more of a consultant and adviser than an authority figure who is setting limits and providing consequences. Give your child this opportunity to regulate himself, including the chance to make his own mistakes.

This process should begin in early adolescence and continue to unfold until your child leaves for college or moves into the workforce. By the time she is 17, you should be almost fully into your adviser role. You should give advice, especially when she asks for it. On the other hand, you must largely stop restricting, grounding, or otherwise punishing her for misdeeds.

There are exceptions to this rule, such as for serious irresponsible acts. For example, if you found out that your child was drinking and driving, it would be insufficient to simply discuss values. You would also need to set limits on this dangerous behavior.

The following case study also demonstrates a serious dilemma where parents needed to set limits on their teenage daughter.

Holly was a 15-year-old girl who liked to hang out with older friends. Most of her peers were two years older than she, and this began to cause problems for her parents. Dean and Sally were very warm and caring. They communicated openly with Holly and were responsive to her needs and perspective. They felt that she was mature and usually handled herself well with her older friends. She was getting good grades in school and was responsible and helpful around the house. However, one night, Holly called to say she would not be coming home. She wanted her parents to know she was all right and not to worry, but she and her friends were camping out. Dean and Sally told her this was not acceptable, and they expected her to come home. Holly refused and hung up the phone.

Dean and Sally went looking for Holly but could not find her. She returned the next morning and defiantly announced that she was old enough to make her own choices. She said she did not do anything wrong but simply wanted to be with her friends. She said, "I was responsible. I called you to say I was not coming home."

Her parents were angry. They felt betrayed and frightened. They had trusted Holly and now were not sure that they could trust her judgment. They were also not sure they believed her story. What did she really do when she stayed out all night? Had she been drinking? Was she with a boy?

Sally and Dean had seldom punished Holly. She did not need to be punished in the past because she usually did the right thing. Sally and Holly could always talk about issues, and this was an important part of their relationship. Now, when Sally tried to talk to Holly about staying out all night, Holly would not communicate. She maintained a defiant silence.

Even though they rarely used punishment, Sally and Dean saw this event as a serious infraction. They told Holly they believed she had acted inappropriately, placed herself in danger, and violated her parents' trust. They grounded her for two weeks and told her she could not use the telephone to talk to her

39

friends for three days. They told her they were very disappointed in her decision and hurt that she would not discuss the event with them. They expressed the hope that she would start to communicate again. They did not yell but were serious in their demeanor.

Holly sullenly complied with the limits her parents set. She stayed home and did not use the telephone. Sally and Dean continued to worry. Then, one week after the incident, Holly knocked on her parent's bedroom door and asked if she could talk. She began to sob. She explained how guilt-ridden she felt for having betrayed her parents' trust. She said she realized that she had been caught up in being accepted by her peers. She did not want her friends to reject her for not going along with their plan to camp out. Holly stated that she wanted to regain her parent's faith in her and promised not to defy them again.

Sally and Dean told Holly they were proud of her for coming to them to talk and admitting her mistake. They said it would take a while to reestablish their trust but that this was a very good start.

Most of the time, the mistakes that teens make are far less serious than Holly's lapse in judgment. These minor offenses can be handled with a discussion of values rather than limit setting. Once children internalize values, they are able to recognize their moral errors. They feel guilt for their transgressions, which motivates them to make better choices in the future. When a major infraction occurs, as with Holly, parents can still set limits to reinforce a critical lesson. These occasional limits have a much greater impact, since the child realizes that his parent only punishes when it is absolutely necessary and fully deserved. Teenagers will accept these punishments without rebellion, since it is clear that the limit is appropriate and fair.

The balancing act of combining limits and values while protecting the relationship is central to Therapeutic Parenting. It is also essential to your success as a parent. Accomplishing this step is particularly difficult, since you must synchronize your actions with the developmental level of your child. Once you succeed, your child will see you as compassionate and fair. She will respect your authority while feeling able to be her own person. This is the kind of parent you want to be. It is also the kind of parent your child needs.

Key Points to Remember

❖ Your relationship with your child is most vulnerable when setting limits.

❖ Young children need structure and limits to learn values.

❖ Adolescents rebel against too much limit setting.

❖ Gradually reduce your limit setting during your child's adolescence.

Chapter 5

TLC: How to Discuss and Solve Problems with Your Child

Recently, at a social gathering, I overheard a conversation between a father and his nine-year-old son. The boy was complaining that his brother was bothering him. The father responded, "Justin, either beat the tar out of your brother, or stay away from him. You have to learn to handle your own problems." I know this father, and he is a good man. He loves his children and has good values. However, like so many parents, he did not react in a constructive way to his son's request for help. By telling his son to "beat the tar" out of his brother, he violated the basic rules of Therapeutic Parenting—he did not convey his values, and he was not empathic to his son.

Obviously, this man does not want his son beating up his brother. Why, then, did he give this advice? His reaction was dictated, in part, by frustration. He wanted to dispatch his son's issue quickly and emphatically. In his defense, this father did believe he was communicating an important message: He wanted his son to learn to deal with his own problems. However, in his impatience, he dismissed his son's concerns and endorsed aggression as a method for resolving conflict. His advice was based on expedience, frustration, and embarrassment that this event was taking place in front of friends.

It's a challenge for any parent to respond consistently with sensitivity and wisdom. No parent can do this all the time. However, a thoughtful response is particularly important when your child comes to you with a problem. At these moments, your child is most vulnerable and most open to your suggestions and support. When she is distressed, you have the greatest opportunity to help her. On the other hand, if you do not respond effectively when your child has a problem, she is most likely to feel rejected and disappointed.

In this chapter, you will learn a technique for having productive and sensitive discussions with your child. This technique is called TLC, which is an acronym for Talking Listening Connecting. TLC is based on well-established principles of communication and problem solving and will help you in dealing with a wide range of situations. You will see it mentioned throughout the rest of the book. You can use TLC to discuss your child's misbehavior, anxieties, or problems with his friends. It's a flexible strategy that has many applications.

Seven Steps to Better Communication

TLC is a series of seven steps that proceed in a set order. These steps are similar to how therapists intervene with children. It will take practice for you to refine your skills in using TLC, although each step is actually fairly simple. You may need to refer back to this chapter when you begin to discuss issues with your child. TLC will help you communicate effectively and will have a powerful impact on your relationship with your child.

Step #1: Identify the Issue

TLC is a method for reciprocal dialogue, discussion of values, and problem solving. The first step is to establish the issue or problem that you want to discuss and to define the goals of the conversation. By stating the issue and goals, your child will be able to relax, focus, and participate.

Don't assume your child understands why you want to talk. To avoid confusion, you need to clarify the issue. For example, let's say that your son has teased his younger sister and made her cry, and you have set a limit. You have told him to go to his room and not return until he is ready to be more caring toward his family. He comes back a short while later, and you say that you want to talk. What will your child think when you sit down for this discussion? He may think you are mad and are going to yell. He may think he is going to get a lecture or further punishment.

You need to define the issue that you plan to discuss. Explain that you want to share feelings and perspectives and to come up with new ideas. For example, you might say, "Jason, I want to talk about what just happened with your sister. I want to talk about why you mocked her and what you can do the next time you get frustrated."

Remember that the tone of your voice and demeanor are important. If you are angry or upset, wait until you have calmed down before you begin talking. These conversations are essential for teaching values and building closeness. If you are angry or hostile, your child will be uneasy and guarded. If you are calm and caring, your child will relax and be ready to absorb your message.

Step #2: Get Your Child's Point of View

Once you have identified what you plan to discuss, let your child express her view of what happened and explain her motivation and rationale. You should encourage this expression, even if you disagree or don't like what she is saying. It is essential that your child feels that you are listening to her and value her perspective. You should encourage her to explain her actions and feelings as thoroughly as possible. Ask her questions. Get her to elaborate. Take your time in making sure she has explained what she was thinking and feeling.

Be a good listener. Validate his point of view and acknowledge that you understand what he is saying. Don't argue or debate with him. Don't disagree with him—that may need to happen, but at a later step. If, at this early stage, you express disapproval, correct him, or look angry, he will stop communicating. This step is his turn to talk. Your turn to talk happens after he has finished telling you what he was thinking and feeling. Don't be impatient. Don't cut him off or rush to explain what he has done wrong or what he needs to change.

Here are some techniques you can use to help your child express herself:

- ❖ Ask questions that help her to discuss an incident in detail, such as, "What happened first that got you upset? What did you do? What happened after that?"

- ❖ Focus on his thinking and his feelings. "What were you thinking when she was teasing you? How did that make you feel?"

- ❖ Ask her to elaborate on key issues. "Tell me more about that. I think this is important. Can you help me understand this part better?"

- ❖ Tell him you value his communication and respect his point of view. "I'm glad you're telling me what this was like for you. I understand your situation and what you were thinking much better now that you've explained it to me."

Step #3: Show Empathy

This next step is a transition between your child telling you what he thinks and feels and you expressing your perspective. Before you explain what you think and feel, you need to make sure your child believes you understand his point of view and his feelings. You don't need to tell your child that you agree with what he's said. Indeed, you may disagree with much of what he has told you. However, even if you disagree strongly, you want him to know that you understand and care about how he feels. This is critical to maintaining a warm and caring relationship. Your child needs to know that even if you disapprove of his actions or perceive a weakness or flaw, you still love him and want to help.

You can accomplish this in several ways. The look on your face and your tone will communicate a great deal of how you feel. Use your facial expressions and tone to show that you care and that you are not upset with him. Talk in a warm and soothing manner. Pay particular attention to his feelings to show you understand. Here are some things you can say that demonstrate empathy:

- ❖ Reflect and label her feelings. "I can tell you were really upset by what happened at school," or "You seem really sad."

- ❖ Validate and normalize his feelings. "I understand why you feel this way. Most kids would be angry if this happened to them."

- ❖ Summarize what you have heard her tell you. "You think that your teacher has been picking on you and has not been fair."

- ❖ Tell him you are proud of him for being in touch with his feelings. "I'm glad you are aware of what you were feeling and can tell me. I think it's helpful for you to understand yourself and your own feelings. I'm proud of you."

Step #4: Discuss Values—Yours and Your Child's

Now that your child has expressed herself, and you have made her feel understood and validated, you can share your perspective. The goals of these conversations are to help your child grow emotionally and to strengthen the bond between you. You don't want your child to feel demeaned or chastised. This is an opportunity to provide guidance, support, and necessary feedback. Most importantly, it is a time to emphasize values.

Once you have completed the first three steps, you should tell your child what you think about the situation. Identify the critical issues as you see them. Then ask your child about her values. What does she think is the best way to deal with the situation? What values does she think she should use to guide her actions? If your child understands the correct values, acknowledge this and tell her you're pleased. You might say, "I'm glad you know what you should have done and what you need to do next time. I'm proud of you."

Phrase your feedback in a sensitive manner. For example, let's say your daughter has lied to you about a grade she received in school. When you reach this step, you might say, "Christine, I know you believe in being honest and that you feel badly when you don't tell the truth. I'm upset that you didn't tell me the truth about this grade. We need to have honesty in our relationship. Our family believes in that. I know you understand that you've made a mistake."

This feedback gives Christine credit for understanding right from wrong and acknowledges that she must feel badly about her transgression. The message is not blaming or hostile. Rather, the message emphasizes that a mistake was made and why, while supporting the belief that this was merely a lapse in judgment. It affirms that the mother believes in her daughter. It also sets an expectation for how to handle future situations.

When you give feedback and teach values, you must be careful not to lecture or shame your child. Make the points you think are important, but don't go overboard. If your child feels that he has to endure a long harangue every time he has a problem, he will dread these conversations and resist participating. You want your child to feel good about these talks. He should feel that you have listened, been supportive, and have given helpful feedback and sound advice.

Once your child has internalized values, he will know what to do in most situations by following his internal guidance system. You can help this process by emphasizing your child's ownership of the values. Do this by using phrases like "I know this is what you believe" or "You want to do the right thing." These statements subtly reinforce that your child has assimilated these values and is not just doing what his parent wants him to do. Rather, he is doing these things because he believes it is right.

Sometimes, especially with teens, a child may disagree with your values or tell you he has different beliefs. Let your child have an opportunity to tell you what he believes and why he thinks his values are correct. If his perspective has validity, acknowledge this and be respectful of his beliefs as much as possible. Older teens may be unwilling to accept your values and stubbornly adhere to their own way of thinking. In these circumstances, it is not essential for you to "win" and convince your child he is wrong. Instead, have a meaningful and caring discussion about your differences. If you think your child is misguided, be respectful, but be clear that you do not agree.

For example, let's say your 16-year-old son has decided that people are too concerned with success and achievement, and it is more important to have fun in life. He tells you that he does not see the value in working hard in school if it means that he misses out on pleasurable activities. You tell him you think that having fun is important, but you also believe achievement and success matter. You express concern that his attitude may lead to problems in the future. He says that he does not see it that way and plans to strike a different balance in his life.

Most parents would not be pleased with this child's perspective. However, it's very difficult to force a value system on a teenager who is adamant about what she believes. You must adhere to the basic principles of Therapeutic Parenting, even at these moments. Don't jeopardize your relationship with your child over any issue. Continue to engage in ongoing conversations with your child and share your perspective in a respectful and sensitive way. You should still tell your child what you believe and why you disagree with her. However, don't be hostile or insulting and thereby alienate her from talking. If your relationship is estranged, it will only convince her *not* to adopt your values. You might tell her, "I understand that we don't see this the same way. I respect you for having your own ideas and values, but I'm worried about your future. I think you will experience difficulties when you cannot have the life you want because you have not put in the effort."

Obviously, the age of your child is relevant to how much leeway you should give in letting him use his own values to regulate his actions. For children under age 13, tell them they must adhere to the values you are expressing. It is not an option to violate these values. When they are teens, your approach will need to change. Teens are developmentally seeking their own identities. Once this developmental stage is reached, be prepared for more debate. Be more flexible and open to negotiation. You will get more feedback and disagreement from your teenager. Hopefully, however, if you have modeled the right way to provide feedback, your teen will be respectful when he tells you he does not agree with you!

Step #5: Explore Solutions

Some situations will be resolved at the previous step through a discussion of perspectives and values. However, it will often be necessary to take further action to resolve an issue. When your child is struggling with a dilemma, you may need to help her find a new way to approach the issue. Later chapters will describe solutions to a variety of problems that you may encounter with your child. This step will describe some general approaches to finding solutions.

When your child has a problem, it means whatever he has been trying to make things better has not been working. Unfortunately, many people keep using the same strategy to cope with a problem even after the strategy has failed. You want to teach your child to be open to new options and not remain fixated on one method for resolving problems.

If your child is repeating the same unsuccessful pattern, point this out, and tell him he needs to learn to look for new solutions. Say something like this: "I know you're trying, but what you're doing is not working. Whenever you have a problem in life, try to solve it the best way you can; but if what you try doesn't work, try another approach." This message highlights an important value: Keep looking for new ways to solve problems, and don't give up until you find a solution that works.

Once children understand this concept, they become resilient. They recognize that solutions can be found to all problems if they persevere and are flexible in searching for something to make it better. Once your child adopts this perspective, he will feel confident that he can cope with any dilemma. Praise and support any effort by your child to try new ideas to improve his life.

This perspective has a powerful impact on children and is a central component of Therapeutic Parenting. Your child will feel stronger and more capable whenever she tries a new approach. Even when the solution is not successful, she will feel better because you are proud of her for trying. She does not have to find the right solution the first time. Each time she tries a new idea, she has made progress. She has taken an active step to improve her situation, and that is meaningful even if it does not solve the problem. Tell your child, "I'm proud of you for trying something new. Even though this particular idea did not succeed, you'll find a solution as long as you keep trying."

When your child tries a new approach that does not work, teach her to learn from her effort. A better solution may develop from examining why a previous idea did not succeed. Finding solutions should be a joint effort between you and your child. When your child is younger, she will need you to generate most of the ideas. As she gets older, she will be more capable of coming up with her own ideas, and you can play more of an advisory role.

Often solutions involve small changes that lead to positive outcomes. Don't feel you have to come up with complicated and elegant solutions to dilemmas. Think of this as a scientific experiment. Make a change. Observe the results. If things get better, stick with that approach. If things do not improve, come up with ideas of why it did not work and make modifications. Never give up trying to find solutions to problems. You cannot fail if you persevere. Remember that your attitude about problem solving models an important life lesson. If you give up or are unwilling to try new ideas, your child will, too. If you are persistent, flexible, optimistic, and undaunted by setbacks, your child will learn this highly adaptive way of finding solutions to problems.

Here are a few ideas to consider when trying to solve problems or address difficult issues:

❖ Look for circumstances that trigger the problem. Find a solution that minimizes the impact of these triggers. If you cannot find a trigger, make that part of your solution. Suggest to your child, "Let's see if we can figure out what makes this problem happen. The next time it happens, see if you can recognize what was going on that triggered it."

❖ Examine what your child is thinking and determine if her thinking needs to change in order to succeed. She may need your help in learning to monitor her own thoughts. You can tell her, "We need to pay attention to what you're thinking. What exactly were you thinking when you got angry?"

❖ Select a new action that your child can try to make things better. These new actions can be small, such as smiling more or saying "thank you"; talking in a soft voice; taking turns with a friend; giving a compliment; or changing a daily routine.

Later chapters will give you ideas for how to generate solutions for almost any problem that your child may encounter.

Step #6: Agree on a Plan

Make sure that your child understands and agrees with the solution. Don't dictate what you expect and insist that your child do whatever you say. You want your child to feel that he is part of the process and that the plan is his. If he feels that your plan is being forced on him, he will not embrace it as a helpful strategy. To get his participation, ask for his ideas and incorporate them as much as possible. The more he has helped construct the plan, the greater the chance he will use it.

Pay attention to how you talk to your child to accomplish this step. Use language that supports the notion that this is his plan. Say things such as, "I like what you have chosen to do. You've come up with some good ideas. I support your plan." These statements confirm his acceptance and ownership of the ideas you have discussed.

If he is unwilling to cooperate because he sees the situation differently, be cautious in proceeding. Most plans fail when children are opposed to them. Be diligent and creative in coming up with a plan that is mutually agreeable. Question your child about why he may object to the plan. He may tell you something important about how he feels or what makes him uncomfortable. This is a key time for you to be empathic and a good listener.

There are some occasions when you should proceed with a plan even if your child will not cooperate. These are situations that usually involve risk to your child or another person. For example, an older brother is hurting his younger sibling, and he is unwilling to participate in a process of controlling his aggression. In these kinds of cases, you need to proceed unilaterally. Tell your child what you expect him to do and why. Acknowledge that you understand why he does not support the plan. State your expectations and what you plan to do if he does not follow through. These one-sided plans typically involve limit setting. Avoid these situations whenever possible, but don't allow a dangerous situation to continue without taking action. Choose your battles carefully.

Step #7: Follow Up and Persevere

Don't expect to resolve most issues or problems the first time you go through these steps. Most plans need to be revised as circumstances change and new information becomes available. You will need to engage in ongoing conversations to help your child find solutions. You must ensure that the process of talking and exploring options is a positive experience. Make your child feel good about how the two of you work together.

Maintaining this perspective can be difficult if you become frustrated when your child does not follow through in making changes. If she fears you will be angry when she does not carry out a plan, she will withdraw from participating. Don't judge your child or be negative if she doesn't succeed or repeats mistakes. Be empathic to her frustrations and her difficulty in finding a solution. Express your confidence in her ability to change. Explore ideas that will help her the next time. Then, revise your plan to give her a new opportunity to succeed.

What Is ICED SAP?

ICED SAP is an easy way for you to remember the seven TLC steps while you are talking to your child:

- ❖ I   **Identify** the issue.
- ❖ C   Get your **Child's** point of view.
- ❖ E   Show **Empathy** for your child's dilemma.
- ❖ D   **Discuss** values—yours and your child's.
- ❖ S   Explore **Solutions** to the issue.
- ❖ A   **Agree** on a plan.
- ❖ P   Follow up and **Persevere** with changes.

One of the basic goals of therapists is to be accepting when clients fail or when they have not even tried. You must do this for your child. Be understanding if she is unsuccessful. However, communicate your value that it is essential to persevere in finding solutions to problems. Make it clear that you will be patient, flexible, and supportive, but that you expect her to continue to make changes until things are better.

Fine-Tuning Your TLC

Here are some pointers for polishing your skills when discussing issues using TLC These are the same techniques therapists use for helping clients express their feelings and beliefs:

- Stay on each step until you have fully explored the issues.

- Ask the same question in different ways to get additional information.

- Ask your child to keep talking. Say things like, "Tell me more." "I want to understand that better." "Can you explain that in a different way?"

- Act confused: It's a good way to get your child to elaborate. "I'm not sure I understand that yet, but it seems important. Could you tell me more about what you mean?"

- Use your facial expressions to convey empathy and to show you are interested in what your child is saying.

- Praise your child for how well he is doing in the discussion.

Here are some ideas for how to follow up on your plans:

- Agree on when you will meet again to talk about how your plans are going. This clarifies that you are not finished with the issue until you reach a successful conclusion.

❖ Give your plan enough time to work. Don't give up prematurely on ideas that will succeed if you persist.

❖ Conversely, don't stubbornly hold on to solutions that are not working. Be prepared to make changes, even small ones, to increase the chances for success.

❖ Always praise your child for cooperating and persevering through frustration. Express your confidence and your firm belief that together you can make things better.

The following dialogue between a mother and her 11-year-old son, Sam, demonstrates how to effectively use the seven steps of the TLC technique. This mother was effective in using TLC to work through a problem with her son. Sam was expressing his anger with too much rage. At times, in frustration, he screamed, swore, and threw things. His mother felt these behaviors were damaging relationships within the family. She wanted to help Sam develop greater self-control.

Step #1: Identifying the Issue

Mother: "Sam, I want to talk to you about what happened this morning."

Sam: "I said I was sorry."

Mother: "I know you did. Thank you for that. But I want to talk about why it happened and what we can do to help you handle your anger better next time."

Sam: "I'm trying."

Mother: "I'm glad you want to work on this, but your anger is coming out too strong, and it's hurting our relationship. Your sister is also feeling very hurt."

Sam: "I don't know what you want me to do."

Mother: "Right now I want to talk about it. I want to figure out how I can help and what we are going to try to make this better."

Step #2: Getting Your Child's Point of View

Mother: "I want to understand what made you so angry today."

Sam: "You said I couldn't sleep over Kenny's house tomorrow night."

Mother: "That made you mad?"

Sam: "Yeah. You let Gina sleep over her friend's house. I don't know why you said I couldn't. Why won't you let me?"

Mother: "I've already told you. It's not a good night for you to sleep over because we are leaving early the next day on vacation. But I don't want to talk about that right now. I want to understand why you were so mad. Why did this get to you so much?"

Sam: "You always say no."

Mother: "Is that how you feel?"

Sam: "Yeah. You never let me do what I want."

Mother: "Do you think I've been unfair?"

Sam: "Yes. All the time."

Mother: "Sometimes you get angry over other things, so it's not just about me saying no."

Sam: "Everything is just unfair. Gina gets to stay up later. She never gets in trouble. I'm always getting punished."

Mother: "What do you feel like when you are angry?"

Sam: "Mad."

Mother: "I know. But what's it like when you are mad?"

Sam: "I just can't stop it. It comes out."

Mother: "What are you thinking when you get like this?"

Sam: "I'm not thinking about anything. I'm just mad."

Mother: "How do you feel after it's over?"

Sam: "Better and worse."

Mother: "I think I know what you mean. You don't feel as angry and that's better, but you always feel bad?"

Sam: "Yeah."

Mother: "Do you think we should try to find another way for you to handle things when you get angry?"

Sam: "Yeah."

Mother: "I do, too. I'm proud of you for wanting to change this. You'll feel better if you find a new way to handle your anger. I know it will help us to get along better, too."

Step #3: Showing Empathy

Mother: "Sam, I can tell you are frustrated and get pretty angry sometimes. I'm glad you are telling me how you feel."

Sam: "Yeah."

Mother: "You think things are not that fair and that sometimes Gina gets what she wants and you don't. Right?"

Sam: "Yeah. Not all the time, but a lot."

Mother: "I know what you mean. Sometimes you feel so frustrated and unhappy that you just lose your temper. You feel a little better after you blow off some steam. Then you feel bad that you got so angry. Do I understand things the way you see it?"

Sam: "I guess."

Mother: "Good. I want to always understand how you feel. That's very important to me."

Step #4: Discussing Values—Yours and Your Child's

Mother: "You know that our family believes in being caring and loving to each other. I know you believe that too, don't you?"

Sam: "Yes."

Mother: "You are very caring to your family most of the time. I am very pleased with you for that. The only time you are not caring is when you get too angry. This is why you have to learn to handle your anger differently. What do you think?"

Sam: "I don't want to keep getting in trouble."

Mother: "I don't want that, either. Mostly, I want you to understand our values. When you get so angry, it hurts your relationship with me and your sister. I don't want your anger to do that. That is why you need to learn to express your anger in a more controlled way."

Sam: "Okay."

Mother: "It's all right to express your anger. Everyone gets mad and has to have a way to let that anger out. We just have to find a way for you to do it that does not hurt other people."

Step #5: Exploring Possible Solutions

Mother: "I know there are times when you have controlled your temper. How have you done that?"

Sam: "I don't know. I guess I just walk away."

Mother: "Okay. So walking away may help some of the time. What else have you done to control yourself?"

Sam: "I tell myself that I'll get in trouble if I blow up."

Mother: "That's great, Sam. I think the more you can talk to yourself to keep calm, the better you will be able to stay in control. What else can you say to yourself when you're getting angry?"

Sam: "I don't know."

Mother: "Let's think of some other things. What about reminding yourself that you don't want to damage your relationship with people in the family? You do believe in being caring, right?"

Sam: "Yeah, I do."

Mother: "So maybe you should remind yourself about that as much as you can. You could also remind yourself that you usually feel guilty once you settle down and that you don't want to feel that way."

Sam: "Okay. I'll try."

Mother: "Great. Now, when you are angry, what is it you do that is most out of control?"

Sam: "Um. I scream and throw things, I guess."

Mother: "I agree. I think screaming and throwing are two of the things you need to change."

Sam: "Okay."

Step #6: Agreeing on a Plan

Mother: "How about this? When you get angry you'll try to keep your voice a little softer. Even if you say the things you always say, but say them less loud, that would help. Do you think you could do that?"

Sam: "Maybe."

Mother: "I'm glad you'll try. How about agreeing not to throw things when you're mad? Do you think you could use enough self-control not to throw anything?"

Sam: "Maybe."

Mother: "Sam, I don't want to make a plan that you think is unfair or that you can't do. Here are the things we're talking about trying. You will try to walk away when you can. You will try to remind yourself that you don't want to get in trouble, that you want to be caring to your family, and not feel guilty for getting too angry. You will also try to be less loud and not throw things when you are mad. What do you think of the plan?"

Sam: "I think it's good."

Mother: "Is it fair?"

Sam: "Yes."

Mother: "Are you willing to try it?"

Sam: "Yeah."

Mother: "I'm proud of you for wanting to work on this. Thank you so much for talking to me. How about we talk next week and see how your plan is working?"

Sam: "Okay."

Step #7: Following Up and Persevering

Mother: "So, how do you think your plan has been working this past week?"

Sam: "Pretty good."

Mother: "I think so, too. I've noticed a difference. I'm proud of you. This is an important thing you're doing."

Sam: "Yeah."

Mother: "You did get mad a couple of times, but seemed to be less out of control. Did you feel that way?"

Sam: "I think so. I did throw something at Gina, though."

Mother: "I know. I was going to bring that up. What do you think about that?"

Sam: "Bad. I said I wouldn't throw anything."

Mother: "Right. Do you still want that to be a part of your plan?"

Sam: "Yeah. I think I can stop throwing stuff."

Mother: "Are there any other changes you want to make? Is there anything else I can do to help?"

Sam: "I don't like when you remind me of the plan in front of Gina."

Mother: "Oh. I see your point. I'll stop doing that. Thanks for telling me it bothers you. Is there anything else I can do?"

Sam: "No."

Mother: "Well, I think you're off to a really good start. I believe in you, Sam. I know you can do this. I know you want to and that you'll feel good about yourself once you've finished the job. We'll talk again to see how this is going in another week or so. Okay?"

Sam: "Okay, Mom."

TLC is designed to be flexible and useful for a variety of issues and problems. It will take practice for you to use the model comfortably. Keep practicing—use the following worksheet (you might want to make several blank copies so you have them on hand). Refine your skills. Help your child develop into a responsible and caring adult. Your confidence will improve, as will your relationship with your child.

TLC Worksheet

Some parents like to write down what they discuss with their child. You can use this worksheet to make sure you have covered all seven steps and to record your plans.

Step #1: The issue is:

_____

_____

Step #2: My child's view of this issue is:

_____

_____

Step #3: My child has these feelings about this issue:

_____

_____

Step #4: Our values about this issue:

_____

_____

Step #5: Possible solutions:

_____

_____

Step #6: This is our plan:

_____

_____

Step #7: The follow-up meeting about this plan will take place on:

_____

_____

Key Points to Remember

❖ Use the seven steps of TLC when you address issues with your child.

❖ Remain positive and supportive when discussing issues.

❖ Be empathic and make sure your child feels understood.

❖ Even plans that don't work provide valuable information about what to do next.

Chapter 6

Two Tricks of the Trade: Multiple-Choice Questions and Monologues

"Jessica, I want to talk about what happened at your cousin's house this afternoon," Tracy said to her eight-year-old daughter. She was referring to an incident that occurred two hours earlier. Jessica had been playing with her seven-year-old cousin, Mickey, when all of a sudden Jessica had a full-blown tantrum. Tracy had calmed her daughter down and tried to figure out what had happened. Mickey said something about a disagreement over a video game. Jessica was too upset to talk. Now that they were back home, Tracy wanted to discuss the incident.

"What happened that got you so upset over at Mickey's house?"

Jessica was sitting at the kitchen table with her head down. She was silent.

"Jessica, I think we need to talk about this. Now tell me what happened over there," Tracy insisted.

Jessica shrugged her shoulders. She still did not speak.

"Listen to me, Jessica, you were out of control this afternoon, and I want to know why. What happened?"

"I don't know," Jessica muttered.

"What do you mean, you don't know? What was going on?"

"I don't know, Mom."

Tracy was getting irritated by Jessica's evasiveness. "You acted pretty badly over there. I was embarrassed. You should be embarrassed, too. Now, we are going to talk about this. Do you understand?"

"Mickey grabbed the game controller out of my hand."

"Okay. So why did you have such a tantrum?" Tracy asked.

"I don't know."

"Stop with the 'I don't knows' and answer my question," she said.

Jessica stared at the floor.

"I'm getting angry now. Stop avoiding my questions. I want to know why you got so upset today," Tracy demanded. "Well? Let's hear it."

Jessica continued to stare at the ground.

"Jessica," Tracy barked. "I am talking to you!"

"I don't know, Mom. I don't know."

"Just go your room, then, and don't come back until you're ready to talk."

Jessica slipped out of the chair and headed toward her bedroom. Tracy could not help but notice that Jessica almost looked relieved. Tracy was confused and frustrated. She wanted to have a discussion with Jessica and to get some answers. Why was her daughter being so difficult?

This chapter addresses the most common frustration for parents when communicating with their children. It's the same frustration that therapists confront with their child clients. The problem is that many children do not easily express how they feel or understand how to solve problems. It takes time for most children to get comfortable with this process. This is especially true for young children who may not be developmentally ready to discuss their feelings. Even older children, who are intellectually capable of these discussions, often try to avoid talking about problems.

When children are not ready to participate, they have little to say when parents or therapists try to get them to express themselves. Many children simply shrug their shoulders in response to a question about how they feel. Other children give a series of frustrating "I don't know" answers as the adult tries to explore an issue. When the adults persist, these children withdraw even further. Parents may then become frustrated and angry.

These parents often misinterpret their child's reaction, believing that the child is being stubborn or defiant. They assume that the child knows how she feels but is refusing to explain what she is thinking. Based on this belief, some parents set limits and punish their child for being uncooperative. This leads to an unfortunate cycle. The parent tries to get the child to talk. The child is not sure how to respond and says little. The parent gets angry and threatens consequences if the child does not cooperate. The child gets tense and shuts down even further.

Getting Your Child to Open Up

Talking about feelings and problem solving does not come naturally to many children. Boys especially have a difficult time learning these skills. Boys are exposed to messages in our culture that make them feel like they are doing something wrong if they are expressive. When children fail to communicate, it is not an intentional act of defiance. Rather, it is a lack of skills or a developmental barrier.

Getting a child to discuss his feelings and solve problems requires him to develop a complicated set of skills. He needs to learn to analyze his thinking and actions and to consider alternatives. He also needs to understand highly complex social situations that involve subtle interactions between people with varying motivations. It's not surprising that some children are overwhelmed trying to figure out these situations. Empathize with your child about how difficult it can be to explore these complicated issues. Even you, as an adult, will struggle at times to figure out solutions to these problems. Imagine how much more difficult it is for a child.

With luck, your child will actively participate right from your first attempts to communicate. However, you must be prepared if your child needs time to learn what you expect. Don't respond to your child with anger or punishment if he does not participate fully. An angry reaction will make things worse, and your child will not want to talk.

Don't give up if your child is initially resistant to participating. The techniques you are learning should be used throughout her childhood. They are not merely a quick-fix strategy designed to get through a tough period. While these techniques will help a great deal during hard times, the real value of this approach is the impact over the long run on teaching values and forging strong relationships.

There are some things you can do to help your child learn these techniques more quickly. The first step is for you to take most of the responsibility for communicating during these early conversations. Don't demand that she answer your questions. Certainly, you should give her an opportunity to express herself. However, if she can't, be empathic with how difficult it is to get in touch with thoughts and feelings.

Your goal is to support your child until she is able to use TLC (see Chapter 5, "TLC: How to Discuss and Solve Problems with Your Child") and engage in a healthy sharing of ideas. Until she is ready, here are two strategies that will help her get more comfortable. One of these strategies, asking multiple-choice or short-answer questions, will make it easy for your child to begin expressing herself. The other technique, using monologues, will allow you to model how to talk about feelings and find solutions to problems.

Multiple-Choice or Short-Answer Questions

Most students believe that essay questions are more demanding than multiple-choice questions. This same principle applies when you talk to your child. Open-ended questions are like essays because they are unstructured and anxiety provoking. It is difficult for children to answer questions such as, "Why did you hit your brother?" On the other hand, multiple-choice questions are easier. They are structured since they provide a list of possible answers. The child is only required to select the answer that best approximates his experiences or opinions. If he is anxious about talking, this approach is far less threatening and much more likely to enlist cooperation. This technique is particularly helpful with younger children who are less able to express their thoughts and feelings.

Use multiple-choice or short-answer questions when your child is reluctant or unable to respond. Ask her things that she can answer with one word or a short phrase. These are fill-in-the-blank questions. Even yes or no questions will get her to start participating. If she cannot fill in the blank, give her a couple of answers to consider, and ask her to select the one that best captures what she is experiencing. In this multiple-choice exercise, you provide a range of answers. Your child picks the one that is correct. This will help her analyze the situation based on ideas generated by you.

For example, let's say your nine-year-old son has been reluctant to leave for school in the morning. You begin to explore how he feels and what is bothering him. He struggles to tell you what is happening. All he can say is that he does not feel well. Here are some of the short-answer and multiple-choice questions you could pose to your son:

"Do you feel sick or do you feel nervous?"

"Did your teacher upset you?"

"Did one of your friends hurt your feelings?"

"Does your stomach hurt? What about your head?"

"Who are you most worried will get hurt in an accident: your father, me, or you?"

"Are you having a hard time with any of your subjects? Have you gotten any low grades that are bothering you?"

"Is anyone teasing you or hitting you?"

While short answers provide only limited feedback, they still allow a child to participate. There is, of course, some possibility that your child will select an answer that does not really reflect how he feels. He may simply want to please you or not know his true feelings. Don't worry about whether he is reporting accurately. Any answer brings you closer to figuring out what is happening and helps narrow down possible solutions. Your goal is to make your best attempt to understand the situation and choose a plan. There is nothing wrong with making a mistake and learning from it.

Sometimes, however, even these simple questions will not succeed in getting a child to express himself. Don't persist once it is clear that your child will not respond. You don't want to have a power struggle with your child over answering questions. Rather than getting into a battle over communication, you should try the following technique.

On a Scale from 1 to 10, How Do You Feel?

Rating scales are a form of short-answer questions that are useful for getting valuable information from a reluctant child. Most kids like to answer these kinds of questions. You can use these ratings to see if a problem is getting better over time. Here are some examples of rating-scale questions:

- ❖ "On a scale from 1 to 10, with 1 being very, very mad and 10 being just a little mad, how mad did you get?"
- ❖ "On a scale from 1 to 10, with 1 being very hard and 10 being really easy, how hard is it for you talk about your feelings?"
- ❖ "On a scale from 1 to 10, with 1 being very bad and 10 being really good, how would you rate how you feel about yourself now compared to a month ago?"
- ❖ "On a scale from 1 to 10, with 1 being a lot and 10 being just a little, how worried would you say you are about this problem?"

Monologues

If you have tried to get your child to talk and she will not, or you have asked questions that she will not answer, you will have to do all the talking. For a noncommunicative child, you will have to tell her what you believe she is feeling and thinking. You will have to tell her what you think she should do. This is not two-way communication. Rather, it is a monologue. You talk. Your child listens. While it is better to have an interactive discussion, some children are not ready or able to participate. This one-directional communication is better than not talking at all. It is also better than having a power struggle in which you attempt to pressure your child into answering questions.

The key point is that your child may need a period of time where you take all the responsibility to discuss feelings and issues. It may require several monologues before he begins to understand himself and what you expect of him in these conversations. This is an opportunity for you to model how to express feelings and seek solutions. In time, your child will be more interactive, and the conversations will become reciprocal. Until then, you need to support your child by doing this for him. It is common and normal for children to have trouble beginning to communicate. He is being a typical kid if he needs you to do this for him until he learns to do it himself. I have spent many sessions with my child clients doing these monologues. Eventually, children begin to talk and understand how to participate.

What should you say in a monologue? You should tell your child what you believe she is thinking or feeling. Don't lecture or scold her. Tell her what you would be feeling if you were in her shoes. Discuss what options she has for how to proceed. Express empathy and caring for her situation. Tell her you are speculating, since she is not ready to open up, but that this is what you think about the problem.

When you do a monologue, don't worry whether you are right about what he feels or thinks. One of the first ways your child may start to participate is when he tells you that you are wrong. He will say, "No, that's not what I think." This is a positive development. Give him a chance to tell you how it really is. When he tells you that you are wrong, let him know you are glad he told you. Tell him you understand him better now that he corrected your misunderstanding. This is an example of how being wrong generates new information and can lead to problem resolution.

If she does not correct you during your monologue, that means either you are right, or she is not sure if you are right. Since she may not know how she feels, she may accept your insights as an explanation for her situation. This is also a positive development. She is better off having your best explanation of her issues than no explanation at all. Your formulation gives her a starting point to understand herself and a place to begin looking for answers.

Here are three examples of monologues. The first scenario concerns a five-year-old girl who has been getting angry when her mother pays attention to a new baby. The baby is two months old. When the mother feeds or attends to the baby's needs, the five-year-old daughter gets angry, throws things, and pouts. She has also been rough with the baby. Attempts to get her to talk or answer questions about how she feels have failed:

> "I want to talk about what it's like for you now that your baby brother has been born. I know you love him and like to help me take care of him. I love when you help me. But things have changed since he has arrived. I'm busy taking care of him. I can't play with you or do what you want as much as I could before he was born. I wish I had more time to play with you. I'm sure that's hard for you. I bet sometimes you miss the way it was and wish we could spend all of our time together.

> "I think you get frustrated and a little mad about these changes. I love you so much and love being with you. I know how you feel. All big sisters feel this way sometimes. You will get used to this, and it won't bother you as much. I want you to tell me whenever this or anything else bothers you. You can always tell me how you feel, and I will listen and try to help."

In this next scenario, an 11-year-old boy has been lying to his father. For example, the boy claims he has done his homework or his chores, when actually he has not. Or, he tells his father that he has permission from his mother to watch television or to go to a friend's house, when he has not really gotten permission. He has been unable to participate in conversations about his lying. Here is a monologue by his father:

"I know it must be hard for you to talk about this, but you have not always been telling us the truth. I don't want to embarrass you, but I want to understand you better. I've been trying to figure out why it's a struggle for you to be honest. My guess is that you think your mother and I have been too hard on you and are expecting too much. Maybe you feel that we're always on your case. I know it may feel that way. I'm going to change this to make sure that I don't ask too much of you.

"I bet you're worried that if you told the truth you would get punished. I mean, if you admitted you didn't do your chores or that you watched TV without permission, we probably would punish you. I guess it's pretty tough to tell the truth when being honest means that you will get in trouble. A lot of kids don't tell the truth if they think they're going to get punished for being honest.

"I know that you don't like to lie. I don't like when you do it, either, because it affects how we get along. I know you want me to trust you. I think you'll feel better about things if you can be more honest. I hope we can start to talk about this. It's important to me to know what this is like for you. I know you are a great kid and want to find another way to deal with this. I want to help. I'm willing to try to change things to make this easier for you. I know it's not all your fault. I'm going to do some things differently by not being so demanding. I hope that helps. If there's anything else you can think of that I can do, I hope you'll tell me. Thanks for listening."

This last scenario concerns a 16-year-old girl who has been depressed and moody. Her mother knows that her daughter has been having trouble with her boyfriend. Since her daughter has not been open to talking or answering questions, the mother uses the following monologue:

"I don't want to pry. I respect your need for privacy. I don't expect you to tell me all the details of your personal life. I just feel bad for you. I can tell you are depressed, and I know things are not going well with your boyfriend. I know how important he is to you. I remember what this is like. Nothing feels worse than having a problem in a relationship with someone you care so much about.

"It's hard for me to know what to do in these situations. I want to help you, but I also want to respect your space. I believe in you and know you will do the right thing. I'll be here for you anytime you might need to talk. You don't need to worry about me asking personal questions. I just want you to know that we can talk about whatever you want to discuss. It's hard to go through these things alone. I know a mother is not always the right person to talk to about this stuff. I hope your friends can give you support, too.

"I love you, but I am a little worried. You seem really depressed. Maybe we could just do some things together even if we don't talk about the problem. We could go to a movie or take a bike ride. Whatever you need, I will try to help."

When you do a monologue, remember the key rules of Therapeutic Parenting. Protect your relationship and discuss values. Here is an outline of the basic guidelines for monologues:

- ❖ Do not lay blame.
- ❖ Be empathic.
- ❖ Offer to do things differently on your end that may help.
- ❖ Normalize your child's feelings as typical and understandable.
- ❖ Speculate on what you think your child feels and thinks.
- ❖ Offer ideas of what your child can do to make changes.
- ❖ Let your child know you want to talk and hope he will accept this offer in the future.
- ❖ Provide your child with a likely explanation for her own actions and feelings.

* Tell your child that you believe in him.
* Express caring and affection even when your child has done something wrong.

Writing It Down

Some children are more comfortable writing about their feelings than talking about them. If your child likes to write, consider these options for opening up a dialogue:

* Send an e-mail to your child. Express how you feel about an issue and ask him a couple of questions. Or e-mail your child a monologue. Don't worry if your child does not respond. He will read what you have written.

* Suggest your child keep a journal and ask if you can read it. Ask if you could write your reactions in the journal.

* For very young children, suggest they draw a picture of how they feel.

* Make up a short answer survey with questions you hope your child will answer; for example, "The thing my mother does that annoys me the most is _____." See if she will fill in the blanks.

* Suggest your child write you a letter to express how he feels. Younger children may even want to mail the letter. Make sure to write a letter in response.

Monologues and multiple-choice questions are interim steps. They are designed to help a child who is not ready to use TLC and participate interactively. By using these techniques, you will assist your child in learning to communicate and solve problems. Don't let your frustration or unrealistic expectations get in the way of developing good communication. Be patient and gently support your child until she develops the skills she needs.

Key Points to Remember

- ❖ Some children are not ready or able to communicate actively.
- ❖ Take responsibility for the communication until your child is ready to participate.
- ❖ Don't let your frustration lead to power struggles or anger.
- ❖ Simple questions and monologues are interim steps prior to using TLC.

Part Two

Therapeutic Parenting in Action

Chapter 7

When Siblings Don't Get Along

Pamela had just arrived home from work, but her children were too busy fighting to notice. Her 13-year-old son, Brian, was screaming at his 11-year-old sister, Tina, "You're such a loser. Even your friends can't stand you."

Tina told Brian to shut up and threatened to tell their mother. Then Tina took a book and threw it at her brother. Brian responded by giving her the finger and laughing. Tina charged at him and scratched Brian with her fingernails. Brian let out a yelp and then punched Tina hard on her arm. Tina started to cry.

Pamela was aghast as she separated her children. "Stop this right now!" she yelled.

"He started it," complained Tina. "He swore at me and gave me the finger."

"You started it. I just finished it," Brian barked. "If you didn't act like such a loser, I wouldn't call you names. Mom, look what she did to me. I'm bleeding where she scratched me."

"I'm sick of all this fighting," Pamela said. "I can't take it anymore. All you two do is fight. You're both grounded for a week."

Pamela was disheartened; she felt her family was out of control. She wanted her children to love and support each other. Instead, they acted like enemies and were frequently cruel to each other. She was exhausted from trying to get them to be nice and had run out of ideas about what to do. Yelling and punishing were the only methods that seemed to stop the fighting. However, their effectiveness was temporary. She knew that her kids would soon be fighting again.

Unfortunately, for many families, this scenario will seem familiar. Many caring parents with good kids don't have harmony at home. These parents feel powerless to change their children's unkind behavior. The fighting and name-calling continue in spite of repeated attempts to either punish the misdeeds or to explain why these actions are wrong. Nothing seems to stop the anger and mistreatment. This problem is extremely frustrating because families are supposed to be loving. Fighting and verbal abuse are the actions of enemies, not siblings.

Ensuring that children are caring should be a fundamental value for all families. This chapter will demonstrate how to use Therapeutic Parenting to teach your children to get along. If your children have been fighting, it may take some time before you can change this pattern. Don't despair. You can restore peace to your family!

In many ways, preserving caring relationships between siblings is the most difficult task of raising children. The implications of not achieving this goal are huge. Some children never recover from the destructive effects of this fighting and remain disconnected from siblings forever. In these cases, even when children become adults, there is a lasting hurt from years of mean comments and insensitive behavior.

It is essential that you do not let this happen to your family. Take steps now to ensure that your children remain close and supportive. The changes you may have to make will be demanding. Your children may have developed bad habits that will require much time and effort to change. It may take weeks or months, but eventually you will see positive results.

A Total Commitment

The process begins with your commitment to teaching your children to be caring and respectful. Take this commitment seriously. It's not enough to remind your children occasionally that this is what you believe. This message must be continual and pervasive. Don't just correct their behavior and say, "I told you to be nice to your sister." You must explain that being caring is the most important value for families. Tell them that this is your top priority and that you will not allow unkind behavior. Make it clear that you expect respect toward family members at all times.

To reinforce this value, you must model this behavior yourself. If you yell or call your children names, you model disrespectful behavior. Set an example and commit yourself to showing your children how you want them to treat each other. If you are hurtful in what you say or do, you will never succeed in changing this behavior in your children. Don't let yourself off the hook by believing your frustration justifies harsh comments. This is the same excuse your children use to justify their behavior. They always have an explanation for why they were mean to their siblings, ranging from "he started it," to "she teased me." Accept no excuse from your children for being unkind. Don't accept it in yourself, either. Rise above your own frustration and begin this process by clarifying what you expect and then by doing it yourself.

When you make a mistake and say or do something hurtful, apologize and take responsibility. Model that you can learn from your errors and not blame someone else. Return to acting in accordance with your values as quickly as possible. This is what you want your children to do. Show them how to do it.

Zero-Tolerance Policy

When your children are hurtful, you must respond consistently. Never let an unkind action occur without a response from you—never, not once. This doesn't mean you have to punish every misdeed and give a lecture every time they are unkind. However, at the very least, you should label every insult, mean comment, or put-down for what it is: a hurtful act that is not allowed.

This standard of never letting any action go without comment is a heavy burden, especially when children engage in these actions frequently. Most parents do not respond to every incident, because it is very demanding to react consistently. Some parents mistakenly believe that it is not necessary to react to minor insults or teasing. However, these seemingly small infractions are important because they can lead to more serious disputes. This is why all children claim they did not start a fight. They only remember the insult or physical jab they received that caused them to react. Tracing back to determine who really started a dispute is impossible. Most incidents build upon a pattern of interactions, many of which are minor.

Some parents don't respond to disputes because they believe their children need to learn to handle their own problems. However, most children do not learn to do this if they are simply allowed to repeat the same pattern of arguing and fighting. Parents must interrupt this pattern. Children need guidance about how to resolve conflict. Changing this pattern begins by the parent responding to every incident of hurtful behavior without exception.

Does this sound like a lot of work? It is. Unfortunately, there is no easy way around this dilemma. This problem will not be fixed by taking your children to therapy. It is work that needs to be done by you in your home, not in a doctor's office. To create a caring climate in your family, you must insist that your children adhere to your values. This effort will be worth it in the end. Remember how much is at stake for your family's future. Once you succeed, your role as a parent will be easier and more enjoyable. It will also be more rewarding.

How should you intervene when your children are not caring? You might say something like, "That was mean. Please do not talk that way to your sister." While this comment may not be sufficient to prevent additional unkind remarks, it serves several purposes. Labeling the remark as uncaring expresses how you evaluate your child's behavior. Your calling it unkind shows that you do not think the comment is funny, insignificant, or clever. You are calling it what it is—hurtful.

Labeling the action as wrong also supports the child who is the object of the remark. This will make the offended child feel less hurt and, more importantly, less likely to retaliate. You have mildly reprimanded the child who has made the comment, so "getting even" is less necessary. By consistently interfering with the sequence of insults and put-downs, you will often succeed in short-circuiting the escalation of these insults into full-scale battles.

Your consistent efforts to step in at the first moment of unkind behavior also make a crucial value statement. You are letting your children know how important it is to stop all hurtful comments. Your actions reinforce the belief that every unkind remark is a problem, even if it is clever or made in jest. You are establishing your role as the moral authority who will ensure that this value will guide your family.

Things May Get Worse Before They Get Better

Once you adopt a zero-tolerance policy for unkind behavior, here are some things to expect:

- ❖ The level of fighting may increase at first, so don't be caught off guard or worry if this happens.
- ❖ You will initially feel exhausted and stressed from your commitment to this policy.
- ❖ Your kids may not believe that you will stick with this new approach.
- ❖ It may take two to four weeks to notice a meaningful difference in how your children treat each other.
- ❖ Your children will gradually develop more respect for your authority.

Set Limits for Serious Incidents

If the conflict escalates or the pattern of unkind comments persists, you will need to do more than label the act. You will need to set a limit on the behavior. In addition, you will need to have discussions with your children using TLC Limit setting and TLC were addressed in a general format in earlier chapters. Let's look specifically at how to apply these techniques to this problem.

As you'll recall from Chapter 4, "The Four Rules for Setting Limits," always set limits in a caring manner. Remember that limit setting must be geared to the developmental level of your child. For younger children, set clear limits and explain what your child has done to warrant this consequence. Mild punishment for younger children helps them adhere to your values. For teenagers, use less punishment and more discussion and negotiation.

When your children are unkind, the key limit is to separate them. This applies to children of all ages. Keeping your children away from each other prevents additional harm. This is not a punishment. It is a limit that you impose to stop the name-calling or fighting. You might say, "You are both being very hurtful. I am upset about what you are saying. I want you to go to different rooms until you can be respectful toward each other." This is a strong signal to your children about how you perceive their interaction. It is a forceful way to stop any further escalation.

For serious hurtful actions you may have to impose a punishment, especially for young children. The punishment should be as brief and mild as possible to reinforce your value. Try to make the punishment fit the crime. For example, let's say one of your sons punches his brother in a dispute over which television show to watch, and you decide to punish him. You might say to your son, "I want you to stay away from your brother because you are not acting in a way that is safe for him. Since you punched him while fighting over the television, you are not allowed to be in this room for an hour. I want you to find something else to do, but no television." If you felt both boys were to blame, you would, of course, take television away from both of them.

Punishment is not the solution to this problem. However, it makes it clear that you will not tolerate unkind behavior. Punishment should be used to reinforce your values and to be a mild deterrent. It can make the situation worse if you punish too often or make the punishment too severe. Harsh punishment will make your children resentful, and they will act up to demonstrate their dissatisfaction. Teenagers will be especially put off by attempts to control them using punishment, so only use this tactic when absolutely necessary.

Keeping a Count

Many psychologists suggest that parents keep an actual count of how often a problem behavior occurs. For example, you could count the number of times that your children have an argument or physical altercation. Here is how you can collect this information:

❖ Write down a definition of the behavior you are counting. For example, "Uncaring behavior between siblings includes anytime either boy insults or swears at his brother, or makes physical contact in anger."

❖ Before you tell your children about your data collection, establish a "baseline," which is the average number of incidents over five to seven days.

❖ Make a slash mark on a sheet of paper any time this behavior occurs. You may want to use graph paper to plot the number of incidents that occur each day.

❖ After the baseline is finished, tell your children that you are counting the number of times they do not get along.

❖ Post the chart or graph in a place where your kids can see it.

By counting the number of times a problem occurs, you and your children will be able to see if the problem is getting better. Sometimes, keeping a count of a problem is enough to decrease how often a problem happens.

Use TLC to Find New Solutions

Whenever serious disputes occur, you should have a conversation with your children using TLC Follow the steps outlined in Chapter 5, "TLC: How to Discuss and Solve Problems with Your Child," and discuss the problem. Begin by clearly identifying that you want to discuss the hurtful interaction (Step #1). Give your child a chance to tell his side of the story and express the reasons he felt compelled to be unkind (Step #2). Be empathic and show him you understand how he feels (Step #3).

Discuss your values and emphasize that there is no more important value to you than being caring, especially to someone you love (Step #4). Here is an example of what you could say about your values: "I am very concerned about how you and your sister are getting along. Both of you are saying mean things and fighting. Our family believes in being caring and loving. When the two of you hurt each other, you are not being caring. I expect you to always be kind. It is one of the most important things for you to learn. I don't want to have to lecture or punish you, but you need to stop saying hurtful things."

Your children may need help finding solutions when frustrated with a sibling (Step #5). This is a crucial step in the process. It is imperative that your children learn new ways to handle their conflicts. TLC is the format for helping your children find new solutions to their relationship problems. Until they develop an alternative to arguing and fighting, they will have difficulty changing their inappropriate behavior.

It is actually quite difficult to find alternative ways to deal with a bothersome brother or sister. Don't be surprised if you have a tough time helping them come up with alternatives. Many useful strategies take time to learn. Some children abandon these techniques without giving them enough time to work. Once you agree on a plan (Step #6), encourage your child to persevere. You will have an opportunity during follow-up conversations (Step #7) to make sure your solutions support the value of being caring.

Some of these strategies may require your child to learn new skills. For example, she may have to practice how to express frustration in a way that is not hurtful. Your child may need you to show her how to do this and to practice with her. If your child has been mean to her sibling, talk with her about how else she could have expressed herself. You might explain, "I know you were mad at your brother. Let's figure out how you could have told him you were angry without being mean to him." This feedback acknowledges that she has a right to get angry and express it, but that you expect her to communicate her feelings differently. You need to persevere along with your child until she learns these more adaptive strategies.

Most children don't want to be mean to their families. If they have an alternative way to respond, they will use it. Keep your child focused on the need to learn new ways to interact. Do not give up until he is able to do it. If, out of frustration, you stop having these conversations and no longer insist that your child find new solutions, the problem will continue.

Here are some alternative solutions that you can try with your child:

❖ Teach him to label unkind comments made to him. Instead of retaliating with a mean remark of his own, your child can say, "That was really mean. Stop teasing me." While this labeling will not necessary eliminate unkind remarks, it calls attention to the actions of the teaser. Labeling is less likely to lead to a further exchange of insults.

❖ Teach her to express her feelings. If her feelings are hurt or she is angry, it is better for her to say it than to hurt her sibling in return. "I'm mad at you. I don't like to be insulted. It really upsets me when you say mean things."

❖ Teach him to give feedback about what hurtful comments do to the relationship. "When you're mean to me, it makes me not want to be around you. I don't want to do things with you, because you are not nice to me."

❖ Look for solutions to repeated areas of conflict. For example, you might generate ideas about who gets to choose the TV show or how to divide up household chores.

❖ Mediate a conversation between your children to discuss an area of conflict. Your job is to act as the referee. Get them to agree that they will not be unkind during the mediation before you start the discussion.

❖ Provide a fun family activity or special treat when your children are caring. Reinforce them for being cooperative and friendly.

❖ Help your child to see his sibling's perspective. Ask him what it would be like to be in his sibling's shoes. See if he can understand what his sibling needs or wants. Encourage him to be sensitive, and praise him if he expresses concern for how his sibling feels.

❖ Encourage your child to come to you for assistance rather than responding in a hurtful way when she is upset.

❖ Suggest your child remove himself from a situation instead of retaliating in an uncaring fashion.

❖ Suggest ideas for activities that will build a stronger relationship between siblings. The more they enjoy each other and have fun, the less likely they will be unkind.

These are just a few ideas for problem solving when your children are not getting along. Don't worry if your attempts to find a solution do not work at first. Keep trying. Make sure your children understand that you will not give up until this problem is resolved and they are nice to each other. Once they realize you will not give up until it is fixed, they will accept your vision of the family and learn new ways to interact.

Here is a review of the steps to stop inappropriate interaction between your children:

1. Emphasize your expectation that your children learn the value of being caring.

2. Model caring behavior in the way you interact with your children.

3. Intervene in every hurtful interaction.

4. Label the action as unkind and inconsistent with your family values.

5. Separate your children if they do not stop, and tell them they cannot be together until they are ready to be nice to each other.

6. Set a limit, such as stopping the activity they were doing, if they continue to fight.

7. Use a mild punishment, especially for children between the ages of five and thirteen, if their inappropriate behavior does not stop.

8. Use TLC to discuss these problems, emphasize your values, and generate new solutions for interacting with siblings.

In the following case example, a mother had to use all of these steps to change how her children interacted.

Fay was a single mother of two boys: Glenn, age nine, and Doug, seven. Fay was feeling more like a referee than a mother, since she was spending so much time breaking up fights between the boys. They argued every day. Most days they also had physical altercations that ended with one or both of them crying. She had tried several approaches to change the way they got along. She used a star chart and had them earn rewards for not fighting. This worked for a few days, then the boys went back to their usual battling. She tried a variety of punishments, but these did not work well, either. She felt like she was always taking things away from her sons, and that did not feel right. Unfortunately, the thing that worked best was yelling. Fay knew she could break up most altercations by screaming at her sons. Typically, she would ignore what was going on between the boys until she could not take it anymore or things got out of hand, then she would start to scream. Doug and Glenn would get the message that she meant business. There would be harmony in the house for a short while, at least until the next fight.

Fay knew this was not a winning strategy. While her yelling worked in the short run, it was undermining her relationship with her boys. She realized she was not being a good role model for how to handle frustration. In order to stop their fighting, she was doing exactly what she told her boys not to do. Fay was desperate to find a new way to handle this situation. She felt her family was falling apart, and she knew she needed help.

When I explained to Fay what to do to correct this problem, she was skeptical. "You want me to try to stop them every time they have a disagreement? That's all I will be doing, day and night." However, despite her reservations, she agreed to try this approach.

Fay went home and told her sons she wanted to talk to them. She said, "I am really upset about how you boys are treating each other. I am also upset with myself for how often I have been yelling and punishing you. Our family is being torn apart by this fighting. I will never feel good about our family, or myself, until I make sure you guys learn to get along. This is the most important thing for me to do as your mother. I plan to do everything I can to change this problem. From now on, I will have zero tolerance for mean comments, insults, fighting, or teasing. Acting this way to someone you love is unacceptable. I will never let this happen without letting you know it is wrong."

When she finished speaking, she asked her boys how they felt about their family. They both had little to say. They each mumbled that their family was "okay." She asked if they believed that it was wrong to treat each other in such an uncaring way. They agreed that it was not right. She told them she was pleased they saw this the same way she did.

The next few days were tough. Each time Fay heard Doug or Glenn insult or tease each other, she reacted with a comment such as: "That was a cruel thing to say." "I think that was insulting." "Please do not say unkind things to your brother." "I am upset that you would hit your brother for any reason."

When these comments were not enough, she took it a step further. She separated the boys and told them to stay in different parts of the house. "That's enough, guys. If you can't play nicely, then I want you to stay away from each other." She sent them to separate locations and only allowed them to come back when she felt they had gotten the message.

Most days she ended up punishing them. She made a rule that any time they made physical contact in anger, they would not be able to use anything electronic for an hour. This included the television, video games, stereo, telephone, and computer. "But, Mom," Glenn protested, "what if I didn't start it?"

"I consider both of you responsible for getting along," Fay explained. "I can never tell who really starts your fights, anyway. You both always blame each other. If there is a fight, you both lose electronics."

During the first several days, Fay was exhausted from having to intervene so frequently. She found it draining to hold her temper and not yell. However, she persevered. She knew she had to change her boys' behavior. She had to do this for her sons and for herself.

About a week into this new approach, a big fight erupted. Fay tried to intervene, but could not separate the boys before Glenn punched Doug. "That's it," said Fay. "You know the rules. Everything stays off for an hour."

Glenn became enraged. He screamed at his mother, "I am sick of this. He hit me. He always hits me, and I get punished. This sucks!"

Fay thought about this for a moment and said, "Okay, Glenn, maybe you and I need to talk. The rule still applies, but when you calm down, I want to hear what you have to say."

Half an hour later, Fay went to talk to Glenn. She and I had discussed the TLC model. Fay realized that now was the appropriate time to use it.

Step #1: Identifying the Issue

Fay: "Can we talk now?"

Glenn: "About what?"

Fay: "We need to find a way to be nicer to each other. Too many hurtful things happen between us. I know we can do better than this, and we can learn to get along without fighting. Are you ready to talk about this?"

Glenn: "Okay."

Step #2: Getting Glenn's View of the Situation

Fay: "I can see you're frustrated. Tell me what's bothering you."

Glenn: "Why did you punish me? I didn't do anything."

Fay: "Do you think I'm being unfair?"

Glenn: "Yeah! Doug is such a pain. You don't see what he does to me. I have to put up with all his crap, and I didn't hit him. Then you punish me."

Fay: "So, you think I should just punish Doug when this happens and that would be fair?"

Glenn: "At least some of the time. If I didn't do anything, I shouldn't get in trouble. I can't take this much longer. I'm going to really punch him out next time. If I'm going to get punished anyway, I might as well just give him what he deserves."

Step #3: Being Empathic to Glenn

Fay: "I know you feel like you are getting punished a lot. Are you angry about that?"

Glenn: "Yeah. I can't take it. Why should I care about getting along with Doug? He always tries to get me in trouble."

Fay: "I realize how frustrated you are by your brother and by how I have been dealing with this. I know this hasn't been easy for you."

Glenn: "Uh huh."

Fay: "I also think you haven't been happy with all the fighting, either. I think that's bothering you, too. Hasn't that made you unhappy?"

Glenn: "When I get punished."

Step #4: Talking About Values

Fay: "I don't like punishing you. I know you're a wonderful boy and that you don't like to be hurtful to anyone, even your brother. I know you get mad at him, but I also know you care a lot about him. I think you know that all this fighting is bad for us, don't you?"

Glenn: "Yeah."

Fay: "Wouldn't you rather get along with Doug?"

Glenn: "If he stopped being such a jerk."

Fay: "Glenn, I know you're frustrated, but that's just the kind of name-calling that has to stop. Would you rather our family be caring or angry?"

Glenn: "You know the answer."

Fay: "Okay. I know you want a family that is nice to each other. It makes everyone's life better. I see how kind and loving you are most of the time. I think it's important to you that you be a nice person. When you say mean things or hurt Doug, that's not the real you."

Glenn: "I don't start it."

Fay: "I told you that it isn't possible to figure out who starts these things. The point is that when you are not caring, it goes against what you believe is right. You know how important it is to me for you and your brother to be nice to each other. My job is to make sure the two of you learn this and treat each other with respect. I know you understand this. I just think you have a hard time doing it when you are frustrated."

96

Step #5: Exploring Solutions

Fay: "We need to find a new way for you to handle things when you get frustrated with your brother."

Glenn: "What about Doug? Doesn't he need to find a new way to treat me?"

Fay: "Yes, he does. I promise to talk to him about that later. Right now, though, we have to figure out what *you* are going to do."

Glenn: "Okay."

Fay: "Sometimes when Doug is annoying you, things seem to work out and you don't fight. Why?"

Glenn: "Some times I can take it better than others."

Fay: "Why is that?"

Glenn: "If I don't want to get in trouble, or if I still want to play with him ... like, if I get him too mad, he won't play. If we're playing a video game and he gets mad, he'll storm off. So I try not to get him mad so he'll finish the game."

Fay: "Hmm. So you actually know what sets him off and can control him?"

Glenn: "I guess."

Fay: "Very interesting. So what have you learned? Maybe I should know this classified information."

Glenn: "Sorry, it's top secret."

Fay: "Really, you know what sets him off?"

Glenn: "Of course. All brothers know how to set each other off. It comes naturally. You have to know what you can say or do that is guaranteed to get a reaction."

Fay: "So what is guaranteed to get to Doug?"

Glenn: "Everything. He's easy. You just have to call him a dick head and he'll lose it."

Fay: "Oh, that's nice."

Glenn: "He also hates when I breathe on him on purpose."

Fay: "You really do know what gets to him, don't you?"

Glenn: "Yeah. But mostly I get to him by telling him I am going to get him when he is not expecting it. I say stuff like, 'Tonight, when you're sleeping, I'm going to dump water in your bed. When you wake up, you'll think you wet the bed.'"

Fay (smiling): "Oh, Glenn. That's awful!"

Glenn (chuckling): "I am going to do that some day."

Fay: "You better not."

Glenn: "I tell him that I'll be waiting to jump out when he comes in a room. He better always be ready."

Fay: "Okay. You've convinced me. I can't believe you actually plan how to get to him."

Glenn: "Yeah, cool."

Step #6: Agreeing on a Plan

Fay: "I'm glad you told me about this. I think I know what you should try to make things better."

Glenn: "Not dump water in his bed?"

Fay: "You're on the right track. See why I said that I can never tell who starts the fights? You know how to get to Doug. He probably just cracks after you tell him these things. I think you should stop setting him off on purpose."

Glenn: "I'd rather you take away my stereo."

Fay: "Very funny. Now that you've confessed, I can see that you know exactly what you're doing. You bug him on purpose. Now I realize you do it under the twisted notion that he deserves it and that it is your responsibility as an older brother to torment him."

Glenn: "Right."

Fay: "Well, this is what I want you to try. Will you please stop setting him off on purpose? Don't say things that are designed to upset him. No more threats to get him when he is vulnerable, like when he is asleep. No more name-calling. Please, just stop doing things that you do on purpose that you know will upset your brother."

Glenn: "I don't know if I can do all that."

Fay: "I know it'll be difficult, but this is really important."

Glenn: "Okay, I'll try."

Fay: "Thank you so much. But I have a little more to ask. You know how you do things to keep him happy so he will play with you and finish a game?"

Glenn: "Yeah."

Fay: "I wish you would try to always treat him that way. It would make our lives so much better. I will be very proud of you if you can do this. I know how hard it will be. But Glenn, this would mean a lot to me."

Glenn: "Okay, I'll try."

Fay. "Thanks, Glenn. I love you. I'm proud of you for being so honest and for being willing to give this a try."

Step #7: Following Up

Fay: "I am happy just to know that we have a plan. Let's talk next week and see how it's going."

Glenn: "Okay. By the way, I know exactly what sets you off, too."

Fay: "I don't think I want to know."

Praise your children for being caring. This feedback signals that you are pleased that they are doing what you expect. Praise is an important method for teaching your children to live according to the values you teach.

Once your children start to get along, they will like how it feels. Being caring and cooperative are their own rewards. This is why it is usually not necessary to use a reward system to reinforce siblings for being nice. These rewards are not as effective as the natural ones that result from having a loving family.

The key to establishing caring interactions will be your willingness to persevere. Don't surrender in this crucial battle over your children's well-being. Never give up your efforts to instill the value of being caring. If you commit yourself to this challenge, your children will respond.

Key Points to Remember

❖ Intervene every time your children are unkind to one another.
❖ Separate your children or use mild consequences to prevent battles from escalating.
❖ Use TLC to generate new solutions.
❖ Persevere until you succeed.

Chapter 8

When Children Get Too Angry

"I hate you," Jill screamed at her mother. Marilyn had just told her 10-year-old daughter that she could not sleep in her tent in the backyard. Jill ran to the desk where Marilyn kept her household papers and began to sweep everything off the desk onto the floor.

"Jill, stop that," Marilyn warned. "You're in big trouble." She grabbed her arm to prevent her from scattering any more of her papers. Jill pulled her arm away, inadvertently clipping her mother on the shoulder as she escaped her grasp. Marilyn felt a sting of pain and recoiled, more from shock than pain.

"I can't believe you hit me," she yelled. "That hurt. Do you want to see what that felt like?" Marilyn raised her open palm, ready to strike, but Jill scooted back several steps.

"I didn't hit you. You grabbed me," Jill hissed. "It's your fault, anyway. You never let me do anything!" Jill bolted from the room, but as she left, she kicked the door with all the force she could muster. Splinters of wood sprayed onto the floor.

"You'll pay for that door," Marilyn barked. "And you are grounded until further notice!"

Jill was on the way to her room. She screamed something that sounded like a swearword as she slammed the bedroom door.

Marilyn surveyed the damage: a pile of papers on the floor, a broken door, a bruised arm, and a lot of hurt feelings. She knew Jill was a good girl. She was usually affectionate and responsible, and she was a good student. But when she lost her temper, it was frightening. This was not the first hole her daughter had put in a door or wall. Her rage was destructive. She had broken some toys and even a lamp. She seemed to lose control when she didn't get her way.

Marilyn planned to follow through with grounding her daughter for this latest incident. However, she knew that was not the answer. Jill showed remorse after these episodes, but then she would repeat the same pattern. Marilyn was worried. She didn't want Jill to grow up to be an angry woman who frightened her family or lost jobs because of her rage.

Excessive anger damages relationships and leads to unhealthy family patterns. At the extreme, uncontrolled anger is dangerous. All parents have the responsibility of teaching their children to regulate emotions. This chapter describes the three most common causes for anger outbursts and solutions to help your child regulate his temper.

Cause #1: Parents Show Excessive Anger

Many parents get caught in a bind when trying to prevent angry outbursts by their children. The bind is that parents find the only way to control their children's anger is by getting angry themselves. Most children will comply when a parent screams or threatens. Parental anger is very effective in the short run. A child misbehaves; the parent screams; the behavior stops. Unfortunately, parental anger is usually more effective than other strategies in quickly changing children's behavior.

When parents get angry, they are rewarded by the results. No parent wants to yell, but they are caught in a trap. If they don't yell, the misbehavior continues. If they get angry, the behavior stops. It is an unpleasant but effective form of control.

The obvious problem with using anger for behavior management is that it models anger as a way to handle frustration. While it changes behavior in the short run, parental anger has a long-term, negative impact on children. Children learn that anger is effective and that it is sanctioned by their parents as an acceptable response to frustration. When these children get angry, they act like their parents: They yell or hit.

The first step in teaching anger management is for you to model how you want your child to handle his anger. This includes how you interact with other members of the family, including your partner. Your child is watching how you settle disputes. If you get too angry, yell, or threaten, expect your child to do the same.

By regulating how you express your anger, you will teach your child a better way to cope with her feelings. Your actions must be consistent with the values you want your child to learn. This is a key step to helping your child overcome her problem. Therapeutic Parenting will help you develop new ways for teaching your child to manage anger. If you need help in controlling your own temper, these same strategies will also help you.

Cause #2: Anger Gets Children What They Want

The second reason children get too angry is that it often leads to a rewarding outcome. Anger is intimidating. People are frightened by it and will give in to demands to appease an angry person. Children are vulnerable to using anger as a strategy because it allows them to exercise control over others. Children have few options for getting what they want. They have to obey the rules of adults. They have limited resources to go where they choose or buy what they want. They cannot punish people who make them angry. The only weapon that empowers them is anger. If they can intimidate a parent or a peer, they may get the outcome they seek. When this happens, anger pays off.

This pattern is especially common in younger children who have tantrums. Most parents have had to contend with a child who has a tantrum in the toy store because his parents refuse to buy him what he wants. For some children, tantrums persist and lead to more explosive angry outbursts in later childhood or adolescence. One reason this pattern continues is that parents periodically give in to explosions and reward the behavior. Even when parents only give in to their child occasionally, it can be enough to perpetuate the outbursts.

Since your child may have gotten what he wants through anger, be careful about giving in when he is in a rage. If anger outbursts lead to rewards, he will keep having them. Most parents understand this connection but fall into this pattern anyway. They don't want to deal with a screaming, threatening child. Unfortunately, it is far easier to let a child have his way. Parents feel like they are being blackmailed when faced with a choice between giving in or being on the receiving end of a tantrum.

Don't let this pattern regulate your decisions. Give your child what she wants when it is good for her or when she deserves it. Make these choices based on what is in her best interest, not through a process of coercion.

Cause #3: Children Feel Better After Releasing Pent-Up Anger

Some parents do not model excessive anger, yet their children still have problems with anger. To help your child correct this problem, you must understand why this happens. Children express anger for a reason: Releasing it makes them feel better. Anger is unpleasant. No one likes the feeling. The greater the anger, the more the discomfort. Anger is like water behind a dam. It builds up pressure and seeks release. When anger is held in, tension builds. People seek a discharge of this unpleasant internal state.

Children learn that when they let out anger, they feel better. Their discomfort floods out with their rage, leaving them in a less disagreeable mood. They feel relief immediately. Of course, everyone around them is upset, but the children feel emptied of the built-up pressure. Even when children know it's wrong to be hurtful, they do it anyway because they have no other way to vent their unpleasant feelings. This is an insidious pattern. Once children have experienced this powerful purging of their internal discomfort, they will repeat the pattern the next time they need a release.

If you have been losing your temper, this same pattern may be affecting you. Examine your own reactions to see if yelling at your child gives you a sense of relief. While you may feel better, it is important that you also find an alternative way to deal with your pent-up emotion.

Managing Anger

Therapeutic Parenting will help you find solutions to all three causes of excessive anger. Remember to emphasize your values. Tell your child that intense anger damages relationships, and you expect him to learn to express his feelings in a way that does not harm others. Make it clear that he can let out his anger, but he must learn a different way to do it.

Use TLC to discuss incidents when your child's anger has been a problem. Be empathic with how difficult it is to change this behavior and explain why she feels better after she explodes. She needs to understand that even though she feels better, this does not justify hurtful actions.

Try this monologue to communicate this message:

> "I know you want to handle your anger more calmly. I think you feel bad after you get so angry. But you keep getting this angry because you want the feeling inside to go away. You know that if you explode, you will get some relief from this feeling. That's one reason you let out so much anger. I know you also feel better when you get what you want. That's the other reason you get so mad. Sometimes you bully me or someone else to give in to you. I want you to learn a new way to express your feelings and get things you want. But I don't want you to use outbursts to do this. Let's talk about a different way for you to handle your feelings."

The key to teaching anger management is finding alternative ways to cope with feelings. Help your child realize that coping with anger will make him feel better about himself and lead to better relationships. In the long run, he will also be more effective in getting his needs met. Your child will require your support in making these changes. His way of venting anger works for him. Learning new methods will take time, and he will need to cope with mounting anger without his usual method for discharge. Prepare him for how hard he will have work to resist outbursts. Whenever he is successful, make sure to tell him how proud you are for handling his anger appropriately.

The most common suggestions given to people with anger-management problems include walking away, taking deep breaths and counting to 10, or delaying the outburst in some other way. These techniques are useful, and you should suggest them to your child. However, these techniques are far from a cure-all. They may occasionally deflect an episode, but they do not remediate the underlying causes. The solution for your child must include getting relief from the internal, unpleasant build-up of emotion. Walking away or counting will give her a brief reprieve, but will not change her emotional state.

Things *Not* to Do About Anger

Here are some things to avoid when responding to your child's anger. Don't ...

❖ Tell him to let his anger out by hitting an object such as a pillow. Children should never see hitting as an acceptable way to express anger.

❖ Hit her as punishment for aggression or to "show her how it feels."

❖ Tell him that it is okay to hit a sibling in response to being hit first.

❖ Make her feel like a wimp if she refuses to fight with another child.

Two Key Techniques for Managing Anger

Learning to control anger is difficult for children at any age. Younger children will be helped the most by your modeling appropriate anger management and by calm limit setting. As your child gets older, however, he will be able to learn additional skills for regulating his feelings.

One of the more challenging techniques for a child to learn to regulate his anger is teaching him to control his thinking. This strategy is based on a therapeutic approach called Cognitive Behavior Therapy. Therapeutic Parenting uses many ideas from Cognitive Behavior Therapy, especially in this chapter. The basic idea is that, to change feelings or behavior, it is essential to change thinking. These techniques are difficult to use with very young children. Typically, only children seven and older can begin to make good use of these skills.

The second key technique for managing anger concerns learning alternative ways to express feelings. This set of techniques is appropriate for all children from the time they begin to use language to express their feelings and needs.

Controlling Thoughts That Lead to Outbursts

The first technique for learning anger management involves teaching your child to change her thinking. This is the crucial link in learning to dissipate anger without outbursts. People who control their anger do so by what they say to themselves when they are upset. These people "talk themselves down." The opposite is true of people who are explosive. These people incite themselves to riot.

Let's look at this difference in thinking styles by examining how two children might react to the same situation. In this scenario, a child wants to stay up later than usual to watch a TV show. His mother has said no because it is a school night. A child who loses his temper may think like this: "I have to watch this show. I can't believe she said I couldn't. I'm going to watch it whether she likes it or not. She is such a jerk. There is no reason she can't let me. Screw this. I'm not going to take it. I'm sick of her. I'm putting on the TV, to hell with her."

These thoughts are powerful. Each thought generates more anger. This is how people incite themselves through their thought processes. The result is an explosion.

Compare this style of thinking to that of a child who controls her anger: "I really wanted to watch that show. I wonder if I can get her to change her mind. Maybe I can tell her that I'll go to bed earlier tomorrow. I can tape it if I have to, but I'd rather stay up. Oh man, I hope she'll let me. I'll be bummed if I miss it. But I can't afford to get grounded. I want to go to the mall on Saturday with my friends."

This thinking is more adaptive. It reflects disappointment, but not outrage. It considers alternative solutions and the consequences of handling the situation poorly.

When you use TLC to have a discussion with your child about his anger, ask him what he was thinking before he exploded. Through a series of conversations, show him how his thinking causes him to lose control of his feelings. Be patient with this process. Your child will not understand the impact of these conversations right away. He may not be aware of what he is thinking when he is angry. He may say, "I wasn't thinking anything. I was just angry." He may not be able to remember or express what he was thinking.

You may need to use multiple-choice questions or monologues to help her (see Chapter 6, "Two Tricks of the Trade: Multiple-Choice Questions and Monologues"). Here is a sample monologue: "I know it's hard to remember what you're thinking when you get mad. But it's very important that you learn to do this. From now on, whenever you get angry, pay attention to your thinking. See what thoughts make you feel so angry. You may be thinking of swearing, getting revenge, breaking things, or just thinking you can't take it. As long as you think in angry ways, you will let out too much anger. You can control your anger by learning to control how you think. This is the most important thing to remember. I know this is confusing and difficult. I also know you want to change this because you value being caring to others. We'll work on your thinking together until you are better at controlling your anger."

This monologue reflects several important aspects to changing thought processes. Be aware of these elements so you can help your child develop this important skill. Extreme outbursts are inconsistent with your values. Your monologues should always reflect values and support caring interactions.

Children have to learn to monitor their thinking before they can change it. This takes practice and is especially challenging for young children. Instruct your child to begin to monitor his thinking.

Monitoring thoughts is particularly hard when children are angry. They have little patience when their blood is boiling. Be empathic about this dilemma, but encourage your child to keep trying until he succeeds. Teach him that feelings and behavior come from thoughts. Once he learns to control his thinking he will be able to change how he feels and what he does.

Some children are not aware of any thoughts when they are angry. They just "feel mad." Let your child know that these thoughts exist even when she is not aware of them. These thoughts may be out of awareness, but still control behavior. For example, a child who breaks things may not think, "I'm going to break that toy." However, she does think it is an acceptable action at the time, or she would not do it. She will continue to break things until she believes her actions are unacceptable.

It is only half the process to develop awareness of the thinking that leads to anger. These anger-producing thoughts have to be replaced with thinking that settles the child down. You can probably soothe your child by talking to him. He needs to learn to talk to himself in a way that does the same thing. Thinking is a form of self-instruction. It is set of directions to follow. If the directions call for temper outbursts, the person will act that way. If the directions call for calm and rational actions, the person will manage his feelings more effectively. Teach your child to instruct himself to manage his feelings.

Your child needs to replace the thoughts that make her excessively angry with thoughts that will help her cope and find more adaptive solutions. Give her ideas of how she can think differently. Show her how this new thinking will make her feel less angry and more in control. The unpleasant build-up of feelings can be regulated by this process. When she learns to think differently, she will not feel extreme anger and will be able to make better decisions when she is frustrated.

There are several kinds of thought patterns that will help him. Here are suggestions you can give your child to help change his thinking:

- ❖ Remind himself of the consequences of getting too angry: "I don't want to get in trouble."

- ❖ Catch problem thoughts as they occur and label them: "I can't keep thinking that I want to get even. That is just the kind of thought that gets me in trouble. I have to stop thinking like that."

- ❖ Remind herself of her goal: "I want to stop getting so angry. I need to handle this better."

- ❖ Praise himself when he is successful: "That's better. That's how I want to think. I may be getting somewhere. I like that."

- ❖ Think of alternatives to having an outburst: "I need to do something else before I lose it completely. I think I'll take a walk until I cool off."

- ❖ Remember her values: "I don't want to be this way. It's not right to hurt other people. I always feel guilty later. I need to do the right thing."

Children find it difficult to make these changes in their thinking. However, the payoff is enormous once they succeed. They feel a sense of accomplishment and confidence that they are in control of themselves. They also have the satisfaction that they are acting in accordance with the values you are teaching. Persevere in developing this skill with your child. Use TLC to have follow-up conversations to evaluate how your child's thinking is affecting his behavior. Support his attempts to change and be patient while he learns this skill.

Questions to Ask Your Child Once He Calms Down

Here are some questions to ask your child when discussing an incident in which he has lost her temper:

* ❖ "How do you feel about how you handled your anger?"
* ❖ "What do you regret about how you acted when you were angry?"
* ❖ "What helps calm you down when you are angry?"
* ❖ "What can I do the next time to help you calm down?"
* ❖ "What were you thinking when you were angry?"
* ❖ "How do you think those thoughts affected you?"
* ❖ "What do you want to think the next time you get angry?"
* ❖ "How else could you have expressed your feelings?"

Learning Appropriate Ways to Express Anger

The second key component to managing anger is communication. Your child has to learn to express how he feels using appropriate language and emotion. Angry outbursts serve several purposes, one of which is to let others know how a person feels. While a tantrum is an extreme form of communication, it does relate a message. Your child wants you to know that he is upset. He needs your help in finding a better way to tell you.

Let your child know that you want to know how she feels. Encourage her to express herself. Validate her feelings and acknowledge that it's okay to get angry. However, tell her she needs to develop a less intense method for expressing her emotions. The goal is not to stop her communication but to refine the style. When you problem solve with her, focus on how she can communicate her anger while still being considerate of others.

Sometimes a few small corrections in style make a difference. Encourage your child to try a few simple changes the next time he is angry. Here are some ideas that might help:

* Try to talk softly when angry. Even if she says the same things, but in a quieter voice, her anger will appear less intense.
* Do not make threats.
* Do not swear.
* Do not pick up any objects.
* Do not make threatening gestures like finger-pointing, clenched fists, or getting too close physically.
* State the feeling in words. "I am really mad. I am so upset that you won't let me go the party."
* Do not blame others or say mean things about them.

When you are problem solving using TLC, encourage your child to try one of these ideas. He doesn't have to do all of them at once. Praise him for being willing to try any of these ideas. When you have follow-up discussions, evaluate if he has been able to change the one thing he agreed to try. Then, see what he wants to do next. Let him build on his success by taking small steps and slowly changing his style of communicating anger.

If she is successful, praise her even if she is still not fully in control. For example, if your child agrees not to swear, tell her, "I am proud of you for not swearing when you were angry. I could tell that you were really mad. But you said that you were not going to swear, and you did not. Way to go! Let's talk about what to change next so you can keep improving." This supports her changes, allows her to move at a pace she can handle, but clarifies there is still more work ahead.

Let's review what you can do to help your child learn to control his anger:

1. Model appropriate anger expression.

2. Clarify your value that you want her to express her anger in a way that protects relationships.

3. Set appropriate limits for outbursts, and do not reward anger by letting your child get what he wants from a tantrum.

4. Explain how the build-up of anger is unpleasant and that she is seeking relief. Use TLC to generate new ways to vent intense feelings.

5. Teach him to monitor and then change the thinking that leads to intense anger.

6. Encourage her to use new styles of communicating when she is angry.

7. Be patient and let his skills develop over time.

Matt was an excellent baseball player during his last year of Little League. He wanted to make the all-star team. He had high expectations for his performance. When he made an error or struck out, he had little tolerance for his lack of success. His father, Ben, was concerned by Matt's growing displays of anger on the field. Matt had begun to stomp back to the dugout after he struck out. He would swear under his breath and sulk until his next turn at bat.

His coach gave him feedback about this behavior, but Matt continued to get angry. His anger would last long after the game was over. The ride home after a game was tense. Matt would rail about the umpires and the play of his teammates. He would yell about his mistakes and call himself names denigrating his abilities. Ben would usually try to encourage Matt after a game, but eventually they would argue. Ben was not happy with his son's attitude. He threatened to pull Matt off the team if he continued to get so angry. Matt would yell that he didn't care what his father did. After most games, each would end up screaming, and Matt would be punished for the night.

The situation became more serious after a game in which Matt struck out twice. After the second time, he pounded his bat on the ground and flung it toward the dugout. The bat narrowly missed the next batter, who was on his way to the plate. His coach was furious. He benched Matt for the rest of that game and suspended him for the next game as well. The ride home was explosive. Matt was upset by his strikeouts and being benched.

Ben was outraged by his son's dangerous act. He screamed at Matt, "I have never been so disappointed in you in my life. It's too bad you played lousy. You probably won't make all-stars. Well, the way you act, no coach would want you on all-stars, anyway. Then, to top it off, you endangered your teammate. Great! You are grounded for a week."

A couple of days later, Ben had cooled down. He knew he needed to help his son. He was ready to try a new approach and was open to using Therapeutic Parenting. He began by looking at the values he was communicating to Matt. He wanted his son to learn good sportsmanship and to handle his anger appropriately. However, he had not spoken directly to Matt about these values.

The fact was that Ben also wanted Matt to make all-stars. Ben had talked to Matt at great length about baseball and how to improve his game. He had told his son many times how proud he was when Matt played well. He had often criticized Matt for mistakes on the field in an attempt to help him become a better player.

Ben had never talked about his values regarding his son's demeanor on the field. As he thought about the messages he had communicated, Ben realized he had not stressed the right things. He had focused on improving his son's playing abilities. While Ben yelled and punished Matt for poor sportsmanship, he had never said he would be the most proud of his son for being a good sport.

Ben also examined what he was teaching Matt about handling anger. The car rides home were brutal. Father and son were both so tense and angry. Their relationship was suffering from these exchanges. Ben's attempts to correct

115

Matt's behavior were doing additional damage. Ben was screaming and punishing so often that their relationship remained strained for days after a game. Each felt mounting tension as a game approached. This was no way for a father and son to treat each other.

Ben told Matt it was time they talked. Matt was resistant. Ben said, "Well, I have some things to say. I know how much you want to make all-stars. I will be happy for you and proud if you make the team. But the way you handle your frustration and anger is more important to me than making the team. I don't think I have done a good job of explaining this to you.

"Managing your anger and being a good sport are values that are more important than being an all-star. If you make the team but are always getting angry and blaming everyone else for mistakes, I will not feel you have been successful. On the other hand, if you handle your feelings well and support your teammates, I will be proud of you even if you don't make all-stars.

"I think I have spent too much time emphasizing how you play the game and not enough time talking about the importance of how you handle yourself on the field. From now on, we both need to keep our values in order. I expect you to manage your temper when you make an error or strike out. I don't want any more outbursts or tantrums. I will be thrilled with you if are a good sport even if you get no hits and make three errors. I will be unhappy with your performance if you are a poor sport, even if you hit two home runs."

Matt had little to say about his father's monologue. He mumbled that he would try to handle his feelings better. The next game started well for Matt. He got a base hit his first time up to the plate. In the third inning, however, things began to go badly. He made an error in the field. He looked a bit distressed, but he did not come unglued. Ben noticed he looked sad, but overall Matt handled the mistake better than usual. Ben was optimistic that the monologue had helped.

When Matt came to bat the next inning, he struck out with the bases loaded. He walked slowly back to the dugout. Ben watched to see if Matt threw his bat or helmet. He did not. Matt disappeared into the dugout. Ben felt awful that

Matt had struck out at such a crucial moment. He knew he had to fight his temptation to tell Matt what he did wrong that led to the strikeout. He watched for Matt to exit the dugout and return to the field so Ben could give him a thumbs-up for encouragement. All the other players were going to their positions, but Matt was nowhere to be seen. Finally, another player came out, but it was not Matt.

Ben made his way toward the dugout to see why Matt was no longer in the game. Maybe the coach had pulled him out of the game because he struck out? Matt was sitting at the end of the bench with his hat pulled over his face. His shoulders were hunched forward. He was crying. The coach saw Ben and explained, "Matt didn't want to go back out. He was too upset about striking out. I tried to get him to stay in the game, but he didn't want to play."

As they walked to the car, Ben reminded himself that he wanted to react the right way to Matt's pain. They got into the car. Matt still had his hat pulled down over his eyes. Ben said, "I'm proud of you for not throwing your bat. I'm proud that you didn't get angry and yell at anyone. I think that is a good start in learning to handle your feelings better." Matt didn't say a word. Ben was tempted to say more about the game, Matt's crying, and the strikeout. He decided it was best to give Matt some space. They drove home in silence. Ben felt relieved when they got home. At least this car ride did not end up with them yelling at each other.

Two days later, Matt came to Ben and asked if they could talk. "I think I want to quit the team," he said, tears welling in his eyes. "I don't think I can take it. I don't know what else to do. I just get too frustrated and angry."

Ben felt so sad for Matt. "I know how hard this is for you. You are a great kid and a fine player. I would rather you played even if you struck out every time you were at bat, as long as you walked back to the dugout with your head high. If you need help in how to do that, we can work on it together."

Matt was ready to communicate. Ben used TLC to work out a plan for how Matt could handle his feelings. Matt began to realize that his own thinking was the greatest obstacle. Each time he made an error or struck out, he started to think, "Now I'll never make all-stars. I can't believe that I screwed up." When someone else made a bad play, he would think derogatory, blaming thoughts about the player. Ben helped Matt to see that he needed to stop this kind of thinking and replace it with thoughts that would help him stay in control. The key was to keep reminding himself that what mattered most was handling his mistakes with class. He believed that he would feel good about himself if he could do this. He agreed to try to change his thinking so he was less focused on making all-stars and more conscious of his sportsmanship.

They brainstormed what he should do when he made an error or struck out. Matt said he thought it was cool when he saw athletes on TV who pointed to themselves when they made a mistake. The pointing was a statement that implied, "That was my fault, and I take responsibility for it." He wondered if he could do that. It was the exact opposite of what he had been doing, blaming others and railing about the mistake. He thought he might try this the next game.

On the way to the field, Ben reminded Matt about his thinking. Matt said he remembered.

In the fourth inning, the batter hit a ground ball to Matt. The ball went right through his legs and into left field. Ben watched his son carefully. At first Matt kept his head down. Then, he looked toward the pitcher. Matt pointed to his own chest. "My fault," he said. Then, he held up one finger and shouted, "One out. Play is at second."

Ben could see Matt glance toward him in the bleachers. Ben gave him the thumbs-up. He could see Matt trying not to smile. Ben never had a prouder moment.

Be patient while your child learns to control his outbursts. It will be difficult for him to learn the key skills for managing anger. Your child must learn to change his thinking and to express his feelings appropriately. He will struggle with this challenge. Remember that his way of venting anger has provided a sense of relief and has gotten him what he wants. It will take time for him to give up his bad habits and develop new ways to manage his feelings. Help him to see the value of making this change.

Key Points to Remember

- ❖ Do not use anger to control anger.
- ❖ Model how you want your child to express anger.
- ❖ Do not let anger "pay off" for your child.
- ❖ Angry thoughts lead to rage reactions.
- ❖ Teach your child to express anger appropriately.

Chapter 9

Sad Children

Ruth was wide-awake. It was 3 A.M., and she was worried. She kept replaying in her mind the words her 12-year-old son, Mitch, had blurted out as he went to bed: "I wish I was dead." Ruth tried to reassure herself that he would never hurt himself. But why did he say it? Was he really that unhappy?

Mitch had seemed distracted lately. His grades had slipped since his last report card. He was spending a lot of time watching TV. He didn't seem to have much energy or motivation. He used to love to play outside and build things with his friends in the garage. Lately, he preferred to be alone. Ruth had assumed he was going through a moody preteen phase. But "I wish I was dead"?

Ruth tried to remember the last time Mitch seemed happy. She had not noticed him smiling in quite awhile. A year earlier, when he was still in elementary school, he was full of energy and enthusiasm. Then he switched to middle school and became increasingly sullen. He did not know many of the kids in his classes. He said he did not think anyone liked him at school. Ruth reassured him that the other kids liked him but that everyone was adjusting to a new situation.

Another concern was that Mitch's father had been traveling a lot. He had started a new job. It was more money, but now he was away as much as he was home. Mitch had complained about his father being gone. His father had told Mitch that this new job was a great opportunity, and they would be able to take a nice family vacation.

As Ruth began to put the picture together, she realized that her son's life had changed. He was struggling socially in his new school. His relationship with his father was less consistent. He was maturing physically. He was struggling to cope. He was unhappy. What was she going to do to help him?

If you have an unhappy child, your heart is breaking. You feel your child's sadness like it is your own. However, you may feel helpless about how to make him feel better. Therapeutic Parenting will show you how to help your child through this difficult period. There is a lot you can do to teach your child to be resilient. You can teach him coping skills so that he will feel confident that he can solve his own problems.

This chapter is organized as a series of steps for you to follow when your child is sad. The steps are presented as a set order. However, this is not meant to be a rigid outline, but rather a recipe to ensure you include the necessary ingredients.

Step #1: Recognize the Problem

The first step to help your child deal with sadness is to accurately identify the problem. It can be surprisingly difficult for parents to recognize when their children are depressed. (In this chapter, the term "sadness" and the more clinical term "depression" will be used interchangeably.) Depression is often masked, because children do not always show depression in the same way as an adult. The classic signs of depression include the following:

- ❖ Sadness
- ❖ Difficulty concentrating
- ❖ Lack of enjoyment or interest in pleasurable activities
- ❖ Problems with sleeping or eating

❖ Physical complaints such as stomachaches or headaches

❖ Lack of energy

❖ Social withdrawal

❖ Feelings of guilt

❖ Helplessness

❖ Hopelessness

❖ Irritability

❖ A negative perspective about most aspects of life

Some children show most or all of these symptoms. Others show only a couple of these symptoms yet are still depressed.

Children typically do not know they are depressed, so they do not tell their parents. It is an unusual child that will say, "Mom, I have been feeling pretty sad lately. I think I might be depressed." This is not how most children think or communicate. Usually, depression has to be inferred by parents by observing their child's behavior.

Some children show their sadness by "acting out." This is particularly true of boys. These children appear irritable, frustrated, and disagreeable. They often seem dissatisfied and critical. They can be aggressive, stubborn, and may also do poorly in school. The dilemma is that many children who act this way are not depressed. These children may have other problems, but not depression. On the other hand, if the problem is depression, these children may be misidentified as having behavior problems and not receive the help they need.

How can you tell whether your child is depressed? Trust your judgment. You know your child better than anyone else. If you think your child is unhappy, she probably is. Observe her to determine if she has the typical symptoms. If you are unsure if she is depressed, focus on the following three questions: Is she complaining of physical symptoms such as stomachaches and headaches? Is she frequently irritable? Is she withdrawing socially? These are the three most common signs of depression in children. Remember that depression is usually mild. Don't be afraid of this label. You need to see your child accurately in order to help her.

Warning Signs to Take Seriously

Serious depression can occasionally lead to self-destructive acts or even suicide attempts. If your child shows any of the following signs, call a therapist or doctor for an evaluation:

- ❖ Threatens to hurt himself
- ❖ Commits self-injurious acts like cutting herself or head banging
- ❖ Says he wants to die
- ❖ Has "accidents" that may actually be intentional acts of self-harm
- ❖ Writes a message that could be a suicide note
- ❖ Talks like she may never see friends or family again
- ❖ Is excessively preoccupied with people who committed suicide
- ❖ Has depression that seems so severe it is unendurable
- ❖ Says that there is no hope of his life ever improving

For most children, depression is a temporary reaction to life events. Depression in children is not usually a sign of serious emotional problems or mental illness. However, severe depression may be accompanied by suicidal thinking and self-destructive actions. If you are concerned that your child is deeply depressed, consult a psychologist or psychiatrist. While Therapeutic Parenting will still be useful, professional assistance is warranted whenever a child is at risk for hurting himself or others. Professional intervention is also necessary when a child is substantially impaired by serious depression. This serious impairment includes a child who is too depressed to go to school, cannot meet typical daily expectations, or is so consistently sad that she gets no enjoyment from pleasurable activities.

Step #2: Examine Your Own Behavior

The best predictor of depressed children is depressed parents. Depressed parents model depression. They don't see life as enjoyable, including interacting with their children. These parents experience life as a burden. Depressed parents lack the energy to attend to their children's needs. They find it difficult to play with their children, joke and have fun, and to be affectionate. They would rather be alone or lie down. Their children feel frustrated and dissatisfied. Depression permeates the family atmosphere.

If you feel mildly depressed, but are still capable of helping your child with his depression, then proceed with implementing the remaining steps in this chapter. However, if you are too depressed to be a problem solver, get help for yourself. Depression is highly treatable. Your child needs a nondepressed, fully functioning parent. Don't underestimate the impact of your depression on your child. It affects him every day if you are tired, irritable, unaffectionate, and sad. If your child is older, he may be aware of your depression and worried about you. If you are depressed, it may be overwhelming to think about helping your child. You can do it, but you have to deal with your depression first.

Step #3: Use TLC to Talk to Your Child About Depression

If you think your child is sad, use TLC to discuss the issue. Ask her if she feels sad. Remember that your child may not be aware of her feelings. It is not necessary to get a confession out of her. She may not have the ability to put her feelings into words. She may need your help

125

in labeling how she feels. If you think she is sad, tell her, but do it sensitively. Don't make her feel there is something wrong with her. Help her to understand what she feels and why she is acting this way.

You might try saying: "I know that you've been frustrated lately. I think you may be feeling sad, and that's why you've been getting upset. Everyone has times when they are sad. I understand how you feel. I get sad sometimes, too. I want you to know that we can do a lot to make you feel better. We'll talk about what you can do whenever you feel this way."

Step #4: Focus on Problem Solving

The key component of Therapeutic Parenting that helps sad children is problem solving. When people are sad, they are less effective. Helplessness drains people of their ability to solve problems. When people feel helpless, they lack the drive to make changes. Depressed people need to make changes, but they are too helpless to implement new solutions. If you are depressed, you will have trouble being a problem solver. If your child is depressed, he will have the same difficulty.

To teach your child to be a problem solver, you must model an action-oriented approach. Passivity leads to ineffectiveness. Be active in how you respond to difficulties in your life. Do not model avoidance. Don't say things in front of your children like, "I don't know what to do. Nothing ever works for me. I can't handle this problem." These comments model helplessness and passivity. Instead, say things like, "I need to find a solution to this. I'll keep trying to make changes until I find a solution. I won't give up until I succeed." These statements model active problem solving.

Tell your child you want him to look for solutions to problems that make his life better. Emphasize this value when you talk to your child about his decisions. Tell him that he will be more successful in improving his life if he looks for opportunities to fix problems. This value is extraordinarily helpful. Once children develop the attitude that there is always a solution to a problem, they become resilient. They believe that they can handle any problem if they are active and persevere.

This attitude is particularly necessary if your child is sad. Helplessness and avoidance will prevent her from fighting depression. Passivity will obstruct her improvement. Helplessness perpetuates a cycle of depression.

Here is a sample monologue that addresses this issue:

"I know you're unhappy right now. I will help you to feel better. The most important thing for you to remember is that you can always make your life better by taking action. You have control over what you do. You can't control other people, but you can control your own actions. I want you to be active in how you solve problems. Our family believes in being problem solvers. Whenever you're unhappy in your life, make a change. It can be a big change or a small change. But do *something*. Live your life by taking control of your actions and trying new ideas until you succeed. Don't be passive. Don't be helpless. Don't avoid your problems. Approach issues head on and find a way to fix them. I'll be proud of you for this, and you'll like yourself better for acting this way. I know this is difficult to do, especially when you're sad, but I'll help you. Together we can make any situation better."

This message is hopeful and inspiring. It will give your child a sense of control over his world and a belief in the power of perseverance. This is the most critical element to combating depression. It is a wonderful value and attitude for all children.

Use TLC to discuss this issue with your child. Be empathic for how difficult it can be to solve problems. Be patient as she fights her feelings of helplessness. Support her in taking small steps toward finding solutions to her difficulties.

What Do Depressed Children Say?

If you're not sure if your child is depressed, pay careful attention to what your child says. Here are common statements that depressed children make:

- ❖ "Nobody likes me."
- ❖ "I hate my life."
- ❖ "I can't stand how I look."
- ❖ "Nothing ever goes right for me."
- ❖ "Things will never get any better."
- ❖ "I am so stupid."
- ❖ "I don't want to do anything."
- ❖ "I never have any fun."
- ❖ "I just want to be by myself."
- ❖ "I only want to stay in bed and sleep."

Step #5: Look for Sources of the Depression

Help your child to identify the source of his sadness. Use multiple-choice questions to help him identify why he feels depressed.

There are countless reasons why children feel sad. Some of these reasons appear minor to adults but are, nevertheless, important to children. Don't overlook causes for his sadness that seem trivial. Your child may be sad because she has to go to bed at the same time as her younger brother or because she is not a starter on the soccer team. Be a good listener. Hear her explanations and validate her ideas of why she thinks she is sad.

Even with your support, he may not be able to recognize the source of his sadness. Don't get frustrated or angry. He is not purposefully refusing to tell you what is bothering him. Many children are developmentally incapable of having insight about their feelings. Others are unable to express feelings in words. They know how they feel, but not why they feel it.

As you explore reasons for your child's feelings, consider the possibility that you are doing something that is making her sad. Many parents are understandably uneasy with the notion that they are making their children depressed. However, parental behavior often leads to depression in children. Examine your behavior honestly to determine how it may be affecting your child. Here are some of the things parents do that make their children sad:

- ❖ Excessive yelling
- ❖ Criticism or negative comments
- ❖ Harsh punishment
- ❖ Spending too little time together
- ❖ Unrealistic expectations for chores or schoolwork
- ❖ Insufficient affection
- ❖ Drinking problems
- ❖ Chaotic living conditions without predictable routines

These actions by a parent can upset a child and lead to depression. It is especially difficult for children to recognize and state to a parent that he or she is making them sad. Listen carefully to see if your child is trying to give you this feedback. Include your behavior in multiple-choice options when you are exploring reasons for his depression. Ask him questions like, "Does it upset you when I yell?" "Do you feel I expect too much of you?" "Are my punishments fair?"

Honest self-appraisal of how your behavior affects your child is essential for helping his depression. Take responsibility for your contribution to this problem. Don't get down on yourself or feel guilty for your mistakes. Be proud of evaluating yourself honestly. Change your behavior if you have any suspicion it is making your child sad. Tell him what you plan to change. This models flexibility and a willingness to make changes because you love your child. These are values you want him to learn.

Step #6: Develop a Plan

If you identify a source of your child's unhappiness, develop a plan for what to do about it. The act of making a plan and then carrying it out is highly therapeutic. Once depressed children become active and fight back against their problems, they become less depressed. Paradoxically, the plan does not necessarily have to fix the problem. Taking action is what leads to improvement. Your plan should be a commonsense idea about how to fix the situation. Don't worry about making a sophisticated plan. Seek simple ideas that may improve her dilemma.

Use TLC to develop these plans and to evaluate their effectiveness. Make your child feel like you are his partner. The two of you should generate an idea and then try it. If the change is positive, stick with that approach. If it doesn't help, develop a new idea and try that. This process is central to teaching your child how to fight depression. The key is to be active and keep trying new ideas until something makes a difference. Make your child understand that all problems can be improved by making changes. Instill the value that active problem solving is the best way to deal with any problem.

Even if you are not able to identify a cause of your child's sadness, you must still be a problem solver. If you don't know the source, make a plan based on what will make her feel better, regardless of the cause. Here are some ideas that help depressed children. These ideas are useful both when you know the source of her sadness and when you do not:

❖ Find enjoyable activities for your child to do. Some children are depressed because they don't have enough pleasure. Since he is depressed, he may need a bit of coaxing and extra support to start a new activity.

❖ Reduce her stress. Identify sources that are making her feel pressured, and create a plan to lower her stress level. For example, she may need less pressure about school. Perhaps she needs a tutor to help her with a difficult subject. Or, she may be overextended with too many extracurricular activities.

❖ Develop a routine that makes his life more orderly. Chaotic lifestyles can be overwhelming. Help him to order his priorities and figure out a schedule for meeting his responsibilities.

❖ Assist her in making friends and having social opportunities. Help her to identify children she would like to see and facilitate arrangements so they can get together.

❖ Help him resolve conflict. If other children are being unkind to him, create a plan to deal with this situation. If he is not getting along with a teacher, find out what you can do to mediate this problem.

❖ Make sure she is feeling well physically. Some children get depressed when they have chronic medical conditions that are undiagnosed or undertreated.

❖ Encourage him to get involved in sports or physical activities. Help him to find a sport that appeals to him and that fits his aptitude and interests.

❖ Give her the opportunity to enhance a special talent. If she has a knack for chess, likes to act, excels at computers, or likes music, find a way to let her explore those abilities.

❖ Deal with issues of physical appearance and weight. Some children don't like how they look or are overweight. Others look great but have a distorted sense of their body image. If your child has a legitimate appearance problem, sensitively give him the feedback and develop a plan to improve it. If he has a distorted self-image, use TLC to discuss his feelings and give him corrective feedback and support.

❖ Take steps to change family patterns that may be upsetting her. If an older sibling is picking on her or her younger sister is breaking her toys, find a solution to these issues.

❖ Offer to spend more time with him. Ask what he would like to do with you. You are probably the best person to make him feel better.

These are some ideas to try when your child is depressed. None of these solutions is a complicated psychological intervention. They are commonsense solutions to problems that you can implement that will help your child feel better.

Step #7: Focus on Your Child's Thinking

Another general area for you to explore when your child is depressed is her thinking. You have seen how thinking is relevant to many problems. Depression is heavily influenced by thinking. Depressed people think negatively. Look for signs of this kind of thinking in your child. For example, she may be thinking:

"Things will never get better."

"I hate my life."

"No one likes me."

"I don't like how I look."

"I can't do anything right."

"I have no friends."

"I don't know what to do."

These thoughts are debilitating and will make her feel worse. These thoughts are also distorted. While she may not have as many friends as she wants and she may be confused about what to do, her thinking is exaggerated. A more accurate perspective would be reflected by this thinking:

"I want to make more friends."

"I want to feel better about myself."

"It will take effort, but I can find a way to improve my life."

"I have my strengths, and I can use them to solve problems and feel better about myself."

This kind of thinking is not exaggerated but is, instead, a more accurate appraisal. These thoughts are hopeful and action-oriented.

Discuss with your child how she thinks about her life and herself. Tell her that she can make herself feel better by learning to regulate her thinking. She can learn to monitor her thinking to identify thoughts that make her feel sad. Help your child develop a new "script" for how she wants to think. Here is an example of what to tell her:

"The way you've been thinking has made you feel sad. You think negatively about yourself and your life. This makes everything seem worse than it actually is. I want you to think more accurately and more positively. I think you should tell yourself the truth that you are not satisfied with how things are but that they will get better. Remind yourself that there are always solutions to problems. Tell yourself that you know you can do things to make yourself feel happier. Give yourself credit for what you do well. I want you to say to yourself, 'I am a good kid who is nice to other people. I like how I am helpful and friendly.' When you start thinking negative thoughts, tell yourself to stop. Think about what you plan to do instead. Remember that I will help you and will be proud of you every time you try to solve a problem."

Tell her to practice this thinking. When you have follow-up conversations to discuss how your plans are working, ask about her thinking.

Remind her that changing her thinking is part of the plan. Empathize with how hard it is to be aware of her thinking and to substitute new thoughts. Praise her as she develops these skills.

Step #8: Keep Trying New Plans Until You Succeed

Remember that persistence and active problem solving will cure most depressions. Do not give up trying to fix this problem. Troubleshoot your plans. Make revisions. Instill hope and a positive attitude that success will come with perseverance.

Rita was a gifted violist, who, at age 14, was considered a prodigy by some. Her parents, Celia and Mark, fostered her musical ability by hiring excellent music teachers. They sent her to a private school for artistic children that was an hour's drive from their home. Her parents believed attending this prestigious school was the best thing to promote her talent.

Each night, Rita practiced her viola for three to four hours. She did her homework diligently. She was a fine student. Her parents felt blessed to have such a wonderful child filled with talent and endless potential.

Celia and Mark were dismayed when, halfway through Rita's freshman year in high school, she seemed to lose her motivation. Her commitment to practicing diminished. She spent less than an hour a night with her instrument. Some nights she did not practice at all. Her grades were beginning to drop, and she was not completing her homework. Instead, she was watching a lot of TV.

Her parents were displeased. They began to push Rita to practice and do her work. They reminded her of her talent and how she had a responsibility not to waste it. When they drove to school in the morning, Celia would lecture Rita on her new bad habits. "Rita, you have always been so motivated. You cared about being great. Now, you are like an airhead 14-year-old. You sit around watching sitcoms and those stupid teen dramas. If you want your dreams to come true, you are going to have to go back to the way you were."

These lectures continued daily but without effect. If anything, Rita was doing less homework and now seldom played her viola. Rita said little to her parents' criticism and lectures. When her parents prodded her to respond, Rita would say she did not know why she had lost her motivation. She would get teary and stare out the window. Celia and Mark became increasingly frantic. Finally, they gave Rita an ultimatum: "We are tired of your laziness. We drive you for hours a week to give you this opportunity. We are not going to keep doing this. Either you start practicing again, or you are going to public school. No more private school and lessons for you. This is costing us a fortune, and you are wasting our money and your talent. You should be ashamed of yourself."

The next morning, Rita would not get up for school. She said to her mother, "You are right. I don't deserve to keep going to this school and waste your money. I'll go to public school."

"What are you talking about?" Celia screamed. "You will get up and go to school, and stop being so selfish!"

Rita refused. She stayed in bed all day. That night, Rita handed her mother a letter. Celia opened it and read:

Dear Mom and Dad,

I am so sorry I have let you down. I don't know what has happened to me. I am so confused. I don't deserve what you have given me. I can't bear to see your disappointment any longer. I know I have caused you this pain.

I am not going to be playing viola anymore. I am sorry for what I have done. I love you so much.

Rita

Celia was furious. What did she mean, she was not going to play viola anymore? How dare she? She showed the letter to Mark. His reaction was different. "I may be off base," he said, "but this could be a suicide note. We need to go check on her."

135

They rushed into her room. Rita was sobbing on her bed. Celia took her in her arms, "What's the matter, baby? Tell me what you are feeling."

"I wish I was dead, Mom. I can't take it anymore. I have no life. You and Dad are so disappointed in me. I have no friends. All I do is go to school, practice, and do homework. I hate my life. I hate myself. I'm sorry I am wasting my talent. I wish I didn't have any talent to waste." Celia held Rita for an hour while she cried. She slept in her daughter's room that night. Celia and Mark were afraid to leave her alone.

The next day they came to see me as an emergency appointment. Celia and Mark had not recognized that Rita had become seriously depressed. As they began to look at the signs, they were all there. Rita had become withdrawn. She was sad. She rarely smiled. She showed decreasing interest in things she used to enjoy. Her energy was low; she was sleeping more and had little appetite. She was guilt-ridden and made negative comments about herself and her life. She felt helpless and hopeless and saw no way out of her dilemma.

Rita acknowledged that she was thinking of suicide. Her parents made the right decision to seek professional assistance. Rita's depression had gotten severe and had become a risk to her safety. However, now that her feelings had been expressed, Rita was able to promise she would remain safe and not hurt herself. She was willing to work with her parents to figure out what to do about her depression and her future.

Her parents discussed their values and beliefs and how they communicated them to Rita. Celia and Mark felt a responsibility to help their daughter reach her potential. They were so proud of her. She was self-motivated. They were pleased that she did not seem like other kids her age. She was driven to succeed and not caught-up in "shallow" social issues that seemed to preoccupy other children.

They acknowledged that they wanted Rita to be happy. However, what if she wanted to change her life and be a more typical kid? Celia stated that Rita had never shown that kind of inclination and would be surprised if Rita felt that way.

Mark and Celia learned TLC They began to talk to Rita and to listen empathetically. At first, Rita was hesitant to open up. Celia tried to reassure her. "Sweetheart, we know how unhappy you've been. We want to find a way for you to be happy. We can find a way to do this. Dad and I are ready to change. We think we have been putting too much pressure on you. We haven't really listened or even asked what you want and need to be happy. Let's talk about what you feel and what you need, and then make it happen."

Rita was finally ready to talk. "I'm not sure what I want. I don't know what to do. I love my music. I can't imagine living without it. But I'm so unhappy. I wish I were a regular kid who had girlfriends who came over to the house. I want to go to the movies with them and talk on the phone. But I feel like if I don't commit myself totally to music and my career that I will be letting you and Dad down. My whole life, you have told me how talented I am and how I have a responsibility to meet my potential. I don't think I could bear it if you were disappointed in me."

Celia was glad that Rita had finally begun to express her feelings. However, it was hard to listen to what she had said because Celia understood she had made a serious mistake. Her own need to have her daughter be a famous musician blinded her from focusing on what Rita needed. She had lost sight of her values. It was far more important that Rita be happy and pursue the life she wanted than to please her parents. The truth hurt, but Celia knew that to help Rita she had to be honest with herself.

"I am so proud of you for telling me how you feel, Rita. I could not be more proud right now if you were playing at Carnegie Hall. I have let my hopes and dreams cloud my values and put my fantasies ahead of your happiness. It's time we start over and figure out what will make you happy. Nothing matters more than that."

"But I'm not sure what will make me happy," Rita said.

"I don't know either," Celia replied. "I know it's time that we make some changes. We'll keep on trying new things until we find a solution."

Over the next few weeks, Rita and her parents discussed ideas that would make Rita feel good about herself and her life. She enrolled in dance classes, which was something she had always dreamed of doing. She joined a youth group at her church. She decided to stay at her same school but left the door open to make a change the following school year. Rita began to practice viola again, but at a less intense pace.

It was difficult, at first, for Celia and Mark to accept that they had been part of the cause of Rita's depression. Once the guilt and pain subsided from this realization, they began to feel relieved. They had been suffering from the burden of trying to make Rita a success. Now they could concentrate on making sure their daughter was happy and on having a strong relationship with her. The truth hurt, but it also brought them closer to their daughter.

The phone was ringing. Celia answered. The girl's voice on the other end said, "Hello. This is Melanie from Rita's dance class. Is Rita home?"

Celia and Mark did the right thing by seeking professional assistance. Therapeutic Parenting gave them the skills to help Rita. By examining their own actions, they realized they were inadvertently contributing to their daughter's unhappiness.

Don't let your pride or stubbornness prevent you from looking honestly at what you can change to help your child. Whatever the causes of your child's unhappiness, show him that change is the critical component to feeling better. Be open to new solutions. Support your child as he changes. Remember that he will feel helpless and overwhelmed at this prospect. Once you teach him to seek new solutions, he will use these strategies throughout his entire life. This is a wonderful gift to give your child.

Key Points to Remember

❖ Depressed children show their unhappiness through physical complaints, irritability, and social withdrawal.

❖ Examine your own actions to see if they are contributing to your child's sadness.

❖ Being active and making changes is the key to ending depression.

❖ Support your child if he feels helpless until he can find new solutions.

❖ Seek professional help if you think your child is suicidal or too depressed to make changes.

Chapter 10

Anxious Children

"Mom, my stomach hurts," Lara moaned. "I can't eat my breakfast. I'm too sick."

"But, Lara, you have to eat something before you go to school," her mother, Barbara, said. "You'll be starving all day if you don't eat."

"I can't eat. My stomach hurts, and I feel like I am going to throw up."

Barbara was worried. Lara had been complaining about not feeling well for three weeks. Barbara kept her home from school for a couple of days, thinking she had a virus. Once Lara found out she was not going to school, however, she seemed to perk up. Barbara wondered if her nine-year-old was using these complaints to get out of going to school.

Barbara decided to take her daughter to see her pediatrician. The doctor said that Lara seemed fine and did not order any additional tests. The doctor told Barbara to make sure that Lara went to school. However, the pattern was continuing. Every morning Lara felt ill but was fine when she got home from school.

Three times in the past two weeks the school nurse had called saying that Lara was complaining of various ailments, including stomachaches and headaches. Barbara told the nurse that the pediatrician said Lara was fine.

The nurse then said something that took Barbara off guard. "I think she is a very nervous kid. When I talk to her, she always looks so worried. Maybe something is bothering her. Have you thought about taking her for counseling?"

At first, Barbara was insulted. Counseling? Lara had never shown any signs of emotional problems. Their family was a happy one. There were the usual minor disputes between Lara and her younger sister, but nothing was happening at home that should be "bothering" her.

Barbara managed to contain her emotions and politely thanked the nurse. She pondered the nurse's comments. Was Lara nervous? Maybe she did have something on her mind and was not telling her mother. Perhaps something had happened at school. She did feel worse in the mornings before school. Barbara also realized that Lara felt fine on the weekends. It must be something about school, Barbara decided.

That evening, Barbara told Lara she wanted to talk. She told Lara about her conversation with the nurse. Barbara asked Lara if she felt nervous. She said, "Kind of."

"What's bothering you?" her mother asked. "Is it something about school?"

Lara said she was not sure what was making her nervous. However, Barbara sensed she was not telling her everything. "I think there's something bothering you that you're not telling me. Come on. 'Fess up. What's going on? I think something is bothering you about school. What is it?"

Lara looked down. Now, she really did look nervous. She was wringing her hands. She looked like she was about to cry.

"Come on, Lara. Tell me. What has been happening at school?" Barbara persisted.

"It's not school."

"Okay. What is it then?" Barbara asked.

"Mom, what if something happened to you or Dad? What if you died, like in a car accident, or if you got cancer?"

"Lara, what are you talking about?" Barbara replied. "I'm not sick, and your father and I are very careful drivers."

"Brendan's mother has cancer," Lara blurted out plaintively. "He said she's going to die. And Julie's father died when she was only three." Lara seemed embarrassed to have revealed her secret.

"Have you been worrying a lot about Dad and me?"

"Every night before I go to bed, I pray that you and Dad will be okay," she said somberly. "I don't want you to die."

Barbara was stunned. She had no idea that her daughter was worrying about these things. She was relieved that she was finally getting to the bottom of what was bothering Lara. But what should she say? Was this normal? Should she get counseling for her daughter? Barbara needed some help in how to make Lara feel less afraid.

Kids worry. Fears and anxieties are a normal part of child development. Most often these fears are temporary and do not disrupt a child's well-being. These fears follow a developmental pattern. Small children ages three to five tend to fear animals. Children ages six and seven often worry about monsters and the boogey man. At ages eight and nine, children's fears often center around real-life things that can go wrong, such as a fear that someone will break into their home or kidnap them. Around age nine, children are developmentally able to understand that people can die, and they worry about losing a parent or other loved one. Older children and adolescents worry about their own health; world events, like wars and crime; and social issues, such as being embarrassed in front of their friends.

143

Most of the time, these concerns reflect a normal pattern of development and pass quickly. Reassurance and patience from parents help with these problems, and children quickly return to their usual level of functioning.

Occasionally, however, some children experience a higher level of anxiety that lasts for weeks or months. These children need continuous reassurance from parents. They feel physically uncomfortable and have trouble eating and sleeping. They complain of stomachaches and headaches. They feel nauseous. They get clingy, wanting to stay close to their parents, and get distressed when left with a babysitter. Some children with high anxiety find it very difficult to go to school; they may refuse to go or to stay once they get there. These worries can be a source of great discomfort to the child and consternation to their parents.

High Anxiety

Many children don't recognize this feeling as anxiety. Rather, they are only aware that they don't feel well. They report their physical discomfort as "being sick." They don't say, "I have a stomachache. I think it's anxiety." Since children complain of not feeling well, parents are usually slow to recognize the underlying problem. They worry that there is something physically wrong with their child and seek assistance from the pediatrician. It is not until the medical concerns are ruled out that parents and doctors correctly identify anxiety as the cause of the problem. This is a prudent sequence to follow. Obviously, some children really do turn out to be sick, and they require medical treatment. Parents and physicians are wise to rule out these medical explanations before deciding that anxiety is the culprit.

As it becomes clear that their child is not sick, many parents get frustrated and lose patience. Parents have less tolerance for complaints once it is confirmed that there is "nothing wrong" with their child.

Some parents resort to setting limits and punishment to get their children to stop acting fearfully. This makes these children feel more anxious, since they have been relying on parental comfort to cope with the anxiety. When reassurance is withdrawn, these children panic.

Parents of anxious children are in a bind. If the parents are too comforting and nurturing, the child may slip into a restricted lifestyle. She may not go to friends' homes or engage in activities or sports, because she is afraid to be away from her parents. On the other hand, if the parents push the child, she may get so nervous that she comes unglued.

If you have an anxious child, Therapeutic Parenting will help you teach him how to cope with these feelings. This process begins with your understanding what it is like for your child to be anxious and why it happens. Your empathy is important to helping him feel better. All of us have experienced anxiety. You understand that even mild anxiety is unpleasant. It is important for you to recognize and express that you understand how uncomfortable your child feels. If your child has a high level of anxiety, this is particularly frightening to him. He may literally feel, physically and emotionally, as if he is in extreme danger. At these moments of heightened anxiety, his mind and body will react as if he is under attack. These feelings and physical symptoms are extraordinarily strong. Children, as well as adults, have great difficulty coping with the intensity of these symptoms.

Anxiety and Adrenaline

There is an important biological reason for these reactions. We all have an emergency response system built into our physiology to help us cope and survive in an emergency. At the center of our emergency response system is a chemical called adrenaline, which our bodies produce when we are threatened. Adrenaline causes many predictable changes in our bodies. It makes our hearts beat faster, changes our breathing, causes blood to flow away from our extremities and into vital organs, and makes us feel afraid. Adrenaline sets off what is known as a "fight or flight" response, since we experience a great urge to run whenever we feel afraid. If we cannot run and we need to fight, adrenaline physically prepares us to handle an attack or ensuing injuries.

All of this is programmed into our bodies. We are well equipped to deal with emergencies due to this adrenaline response. Sometimes, however, adrenaline is produced when there is no real crisis. If a person fears an emergency, this perception will trigger the same chemical reaction as a real emergency. Once the adrenaline is in our bloodstream, we will have automatic physical and emotional reactions whether the emergency is real or not.

Anxiety in children is closely linked to this adrenaline-based system. Some children produce more adrenaline than others. These children are more prone to have problems with anxiety. Whenever their adrenaline system is activated, these kids respond in the way their bodies are programmed. They become fearful, complain that they do not feel well, and want to run away from what is frightening them. These responses are all normal reactions when adrenaline is released. Once the adrenaline is flowing in their bodies, these children feel frightened and panicky. They are desperate to feel better and appear terrified to those around them.

If your child is showing these symptoms, it's important to realize that her feelings are real. While she may not have a virus or be sick, the intensity of her feelings is controlled by a real physiological process. If she happens to produce a large amount of adrenaline, she is fighting against her own body when she tries to control her anxiety. In this sense, many problems with anxiety are more physiologically based than emotionally driven.

Adults who experience strong adrenaline responses often say they feel like they are going to die or have a nervous breakdown. That is how bad it feels. Your child will be desperate to make these feelings go away. He gets clingy and desperate for nurturing because of the intensity of these feelings. When you comfort him and he feels secure, the adrenaline response ends, and he feels enormous relief. His body turns off the emergency response system, and he can relax. Usually, comfort from a parent is sufficient to end his anxiety and fearfulness.

Let's look at a typical example of how this plays out. Let's say your child is afraid that someone is going to break into the house at night and harm her or her family. She will show symptoms of anxiety, especially when it is time to go to sleep or when you are not home. She starts thinking about the prospect of the intruder coming into the home and kidnapping or killing her. When it is time for bed, she will not want to sleep alone. She will ask you to lie down with her until she falls asleep. If she wakes up at night, she will panic and scream for you to come and protect her. If you hire a babysitter, she will beg you not to leave.

Whenever this child feels threatened by the prospect of an intruder, her body begins to produce adrenaline. The emergency is not real, but the child fears it is. Her body responds to the perceived threat. As she gets ready for bed, the adrenaline starts to flow. She feels afraid. She wants to run from her bedroom. She feels sick to her stomach. Her thoughts race. She is unable to calm herself under the surge of adrenaline. She comes out of her bedroom, terrified. You respond with comfort and lay down with her. You reassure her. The adrenaline stops. Her terror subsides, and she falls asleep. The next night the pattern repeats.

After a few nights, this routine begins to bother you. You decide that you have given her sufficient reassurance. You are concerned that she is regressing to more childish behaviors. You tell her you will not lie down with her anymore. Now, she lies alone in her bed with her thoughts racing. She imagines that every noise is an intruder trying to break into the home. Her thoughts convince her body that this is an emergency, and the adrenaline flows full force. She begs you to lay down with her. You refuse. She has now been denied the source of comfort that makes these feelings stop. Her panic intensifies. She is unable to sleep or comfort herself. She becomes so agitated she loses control. She sobs and gasps for air. She throws up in her bed. Then, you feel you must respond.

This is a common pattern that is very difficult for both parent and child. The child is afraid and desperate. The parent sees the irrationality of the fear and wants the child to cope, but the child cannot calm down. Indeed, when the parent refuses to help, the child becomes so frantic that it is a crisis. When their child can no longer cope, most parents will eventually step in to settle down the child. It is almost impossible for parents not to respond to a terrified child. This is an understandable response. However, it establishes a pattern where the child knows the parent will eventually rescue him. The parent feels coerced into responding to a crisis that he thinks the child should handle more independently.

Overcoming Anxiety

To help your child when he feels anxious, you must understand these dynamics. Your child is responding to real physical symptoms that are powerful and frightening. He will feel better when you comfort him or let him avoid the thing he fears. However, this will establish a pattern of avoidance and dependence on you whenever he feels afraid. Your child needs your compassion and empathy. He also needs your help in finding a way out of this trap. Your solution must be compassionate and supportive. However, the solution must also teach him how to cope with these feelings, so he does not avoid responsibility or become overly dependent on you to calm his fears.

Now that you understand the physiological process underlying your child's fears, use the following steps to help her overcome her anxieties.

Step #1: Teach Your Child About Adrenaline

The first step in finding a solution to this dilemma is for you to explain to your child the physiological connection between anxiety and adrenaline. Depending upon his age, you may need to simplify your explanation. Make sure that your child knows that his feelings are real and caused by a chemical in his body. Explain that he feels sick and frightened because this chemical is supposed to make him feel this way. Tell him you will help him learn how to manage this feeling and to control this chemical. Reassure him that he will learn to regulate this process, and he will feel better.

Here is a sample monologue for how to explain this to a young child:

> "I know that you've been feeling sick in your tummy lately. I know how bad this feels. I want to explain why you feel this way. When something makes you feel afraid, your body makes a chemical to help you. This chemical is good for you in a lot of ways. But whenever this chemical is in your body, it will make your tummy feel sick, you won't want to eat, and you will feel nervous or afraid. You know I'll always help you. What we need to do is teach you how to control the chemical that makes you feel this way."

This explanation is important because it validates that you know how your child feels and that her physical sensations are real. The message is also significant because it redefines the problem. The problem is not what the child fears. It is not monsters, boogey men, getting lost or kidnapped, or even that a loved one could die. The problem is now defined as learning to cope, and eventually control, a natural process within the body. This redefinition is helpful because it normalizes the child's experience, gives reassurance that the problem can be fixed, and concretizes the issue to a physiological process rather than an irrational fear.

Step #2: Make the Connection Between Scary Thoughts and Adrenaline

Your child will still be afraid of whatever has set this process in motion. Your job is to show him how his thoughts set off the chemical process that makes him feel sick and afraid. He must learn that when he thinks about scary things, his body makes adrenaline. If he is lying in bed at night and begins to interpret every noise as a monster or an intruder, his body will respond as if it is an emergency and release adrenaline. If he thinks that his father may get killed or injured in a car accident, he will make adrenaline. If he fears a war will break out in his city, his body will respond like it is a real emergency.

Does Your Child Have a Phobia?

If your child has a strong, specific fear, he may have a phobia. Common objects and situations that children fear are animals, storms, medical procedures, and germs. Consult a therapist if the following symptoms interfere with your child's daily functioning:

- ❖ Excessive worry brought on by a specific object or situation.

- ❖ The anxiety may be shown as crying, clinging to a parent, or freezing.

- ❖ The child may try frantically to avoid the object or situation.

- ❖ The avoidance and fear interfere with the child's usual routine or functioning.

Thoughts are at the heart of all anxieties and fears. Help your child to articulate his anxiety-producing thoughts. Show her how they lead to predictable physical reactions. Getting children to articulate their thoughts can be difficult. Use TLC to assist your child in expressing her fears. Some children are embarrassed about revealing their anxieties. Use multiple-choice questions to help her reveal her thinking. Remember that young children may have difficulty knowing their own thoughts and feelings.

Step #3: Interrupt the Flow of Scary Thoughts

Once you have found out or speculated about what is making your child anxious, tell him that he needs to learn to stop thinking thoughts that make him feel anxious. There are two ways to help him change his thinking. The first way is to teach him to distract himself from thinking thoughts that trigger adrenaline. Any mental activity that interrupts the flow of anxious thoughts will help. Here are a few examples of distracting mental activities:

* Counting backward from 100
* Remembering the names of all the children in his class
* Recalling all the television shows she has watched during the week
* Singing a song in his head
* Imagining a pleasant scene, such as relaxing at the beach

These activities require concentration. When a child is feeling anxious, these activities will interfere with the scary thoughts. Tell your child to practice these activities when he is not anxious. Then, when he is struggling to cope with adrenaline, remind him to try this technique. Praise him for his efforts. Tell him that this technique may not stop all the anxiety, but he will notice a difference.

The second way to interrupt scary thoughts is to replace these unwanted thoughts with new, adaptive thoughts. Help your child create a script of new thoughts that will make her feel better. Calming thoughts will not elicit adrenaline. Your child can use this form of self-talk to calm herself. Here are some thoughts that may work for your child:

> "I know this feeling is just adrenaline. I will feel better as soon as the chemical goes away."

> "I know there is no such thing as monsters. I have to stop scaring myself."

> "I want to feel better. I know I can do it. I will feel good when I learn to calm myself down."

> "I am going to stay in school today even though it is hard. Adrenaline makes me want to run. I am going to fight back and make myself stay, even if I feel afraid."

These thoughts are realistic and far less frightening. When your child substitutes these thoughts for the scary ones, he will feel more in control. These thoughts will not elicit an adrenaline rush. The challenge in using these techniques is to employ them even when he is feeling anxious. The adrenaline will signal an emergency. He will have to override this chemical urge and use these strategies, even when his tendency will be to avoid or run away. He will need your support and encouragement to stick with this approach. Be patient. He will tell you that it is not working. Let him know that with practice these skills will help him feel better. Teach him perseverance by remaining committed to using these helpful ideas until he succeeds.

Let's look at another specific but common set of thoughts that you should watch for in your child. Once children become fearful and have strong adrenaline responses, they often develop a fear of being afraid. Their experience of high adrenaline levels is so unpleasant that they worry that it will happen again. This fear is often expressed as a fear of feeling sick or throwing up. These children don't want to go to school or leave home because they are worried they will get sick. They tell their parents, "What if I throw up on the bus on the way to school?" These children monitor their bodies and react to the first sign of discomfort. This sets off a downward spiral. The child worries that she will feel sick when she is not home. This fearful thought makes her body produce adrenaline. The first influx of adrenaline leads to the predictable physical symptoms, including stomach distress. She thinks, "I think I am going to throw up. My stomach hurts so bad. What if it gets worse when I go to school and I throw up in class?"

These thoughts lead to more adrenaline and the process becomes self-perpetuating. This whole sequence is triggered by a fear of being afraid. While the child's first adrenaline response may have been over an issue, such as a fear of dogs, the child then becomes afraid of his own physical symptoms. Long after he has stopped worrying about the dog, he may be trapped in this cycle.

You will need to use the techniques described in this step to help your child overcome her fear of being afraid. Help her see that her fear of feeling sick makes her feel sicker. Remind her that the key to feeling better is learning how to control the thinking that leads to adrenaline release. This includes worrying about how her body feels and what will happen if she feels sick. She needs to understand the connection between her thinking and her physical sensations. Then she needs to substitute new thoughts that will stop or interrupt the flow of adrenaline.

Here is a way to explain this process to your child:

"I know that you're worried about feeling sick and throwing up. That's not a good feeling. I know it's hard not to think about feeling sick, but that's what you need to do. The more you think that you may throw up, the worse you will feel. When you think about your stomach and how it hurts, that will also make you feel worse. I want you to practice thinking in a different way. I want you to tell yourself things that will make you feel better. Tell yourself, 'I will feel better soon. I have felt this way before, and I know it will go away.' You can also try to think of something that will distract you from thinking about feeling sick. Think about your favorite

TV shows. Sing a song to yourself. Try to remember the names of all the kids on your soccer team. Any thoughts that get in the way of focusing on how your stomach feels will help you feel better."

This is a difficult but necessary task for children who worry. Learning to see the connection between their thoughts and how they feel is the key to managing anxiety. With practice, they will become adept at recognizing the thoughts that lead to feeling nervous and sick, and they will be able to replace this maladaptive thinking. Once they learn to do this, they will be capable of handling their fears and worries without avoiding important responsibilities or activities. This is a valuable lifelong skill that will help children cope with challenges well into their adulthood.

Step #4: Develop a Plan to Gradually Confront the Fear

The next step is to develop a plan that attacks the fear directly. This plan is another method for interrupting the adrenaline response. It also reinforces the value of problem solving as a method for coping with anxiety. You already understand that Therapeutic Parenting relies on action to combat problems. Here are some examples of the kinds of plans that help children feel less anxious:

❖ Educate your child about what he fears. For example, if he fears storms, see if he wants to read books or watch videos that will teach him more about the subject.

❖ Develop a comforting ritual that your child can use when she is afraid. This might include holding a favorite stuffed animal, singing a favorite song, or swinging on the swing set. These predictable acts calm children and help them to cope.

❖ Agree to have nightly talks about his anxiety to discuss his thinking and ideas for problem solving. These talks will allow him to save his worries until a specified time when he knows he will have the chance to share his feelings with you.

- Tell her stories about when you were a child and how you overcame your fears. This will normalize her experience and will model coping and conquering fears.

- Practice doing the things he fears with him. If he is afraid to ride on a bus, take him on bus rides. If he is fearful of what is down in the cellar, take him there and explore the area together.

- Expose her to things she fears in small doses and gradually increase her exposure. If she is worried about scary animals, gradually let her get used to them—first through books and videos, then trips to see animals. Begin by taking her to an aquarium. Then go to a petting zoo where there are domesticated animals. Next, move on to a zoo with wild animals.

- If he fears a social situation, plan out a strategy together. Discuss whom he will talk to and what he will say. Role-play the situation with him.

- Use TLC to troubleshoot your plans. Create a plan and see if it works. Make modifications, and persevere until you succeed.

Your child will feel better when she is doing something active to defeat her anxieties. The plan should progress in small steps as your child gradually learns to fight her fears.

Anxiety Runs in the Family

Many children develop fears and anxieties based on what their parents fear. Many parents are unaware that they are transmitting their fears to their children. This process is subtle. Parents are often too conscientious in protecting their children from the things the parents fear most. For example, let's say you have a fear of severe storms and the dangers they pose to your family. Your child may learn this fear by how you react to storms. You may tell him he cannot go visit a friend on a summer afternoon because the weather forecast is for thunderstorms. You may remind him frequently about what to do if he is caught in a storm.

He may overhear you telling a friend about a severe storm that frightened you. You may make a big deal out of making storm preparations in your home to ensure you are prepared if a storm hits.

While these actions are responsible, they also communicate your concerns and sense of danger. While you are teaching safety, you are also telling your child what you fear and where you perceive danger. This communication is a factor in the development of anxiety in children. Most children become fearful of the same things their parents fear. Children see their parents as powerful and capable. When children sense that their parents are fearful, this is alarming. They assume that if their brave parent is afraid, this thing must really be bad.

Carefully examine your own anxieties. Make sure you are communicating what you want your child to learn. If you have an exaggerated fear, do not let this spill over to your child. Teach her to be safe. However, do not teach her to be afraid of what you fear. Therapeutic Parenting emphasizes honest self-appraisal by parents. Your children will take their cues from you. If you are calm and not fearful when dealing with an issue, your child will have the same reaction. If you are stressed and anxiety ridden, your child will be, too.

You have an important responsibility to keep your child safe and to teach him to identify dangerous situations. This is an increasingly difficult task for parents. The world is more dangerous to children than it used to be. It's not safe for many children to play in their own neighborhoods, trust strangers, or hang out with certain peers at school. Finding the right balance between safety and excessive worry is not easy. You will need to decide the correct balance for your child. However, if you think your child has become overly fearful, examine what you have communicated to determine if you have gone too far in pointing out life's potential dangers.

When Bad Things Happen

Some children have frightening or painful experiences such as seeing a family member injured, the death of a favorite pet, or a burglar breaking into a nearby home. When these events occur, children show signs of stress that usually pass with time. These symptoms include:

- ❖ Bad dreams or vivid, upsetting memories
- ❖ Tearfulness
- ❖ Difficulty sleeping and eating
- ❖ Avoidance of situations that remind them of the upsetting event
- ❖ Difficulty concentrating at school
- ❖ Watchfulness, or what is known as "hypervigilance"
- ❖ Restlessness
- ❖ Feeling or acting like they are in a daze

Here are some common fears that parents inadvertently transmit to their children:

- ❖ **Fear of being sick.** This occurs when parents repeatedly remind their children that they may get sick if they don't take care of themselves. "Put on your coat. You're going to catch a cold." These parents rush to call the doctor at any sign of illness, take their child's temperature too often, and show signs of anxiety whenever their child has any mild discomfort.

- ❖ **Fear of germs.** Some parents are compulsive about contamination and go to great lengths to make their homes germfree. These parents use antibacterial products, worry when their children don't wash their hands, and tell their children not to touch common objects because they are "dirty."

- ❖ **Fear of failure.** This fear is communicated by harping on performance and stressing the negative consequences of not being a high achiever. These parents worry that their children will not be admitted to the right schools, receive appropriate recognition, or be placed in the classes for the brightest children. Children of these parents are afraid to fail and fearful of disappointing their parents.

- ❖ **Fear of being fat.** This is particularly common for teenage girls whose parents have harped on weight issues. These parents give lots of feedback about how much their children are eating and how they look. These children are afraid of getting fat. This places them at risk of developing an eating disorder.

James, a sophomore in high school, was an excellent basketball player and fine student. His parents, Alice and Mike, were proud of his accomplishments and his kind nature. Alice's only concern for James was his health. She knew she was overprotective and that she worried too much. James was their only child. Ever since he was an infant, she was hypervigilant whenever he seemed sick. At the first sign of illness, she called the doctor. She kept him home from school whenever he was under the weather. She reminded him to take care of himself everyday. She insisted his clothes were warm enough and that he ate healthily. She was concerned with his fluid intake and made sure he drank enough water.

Fortunately, James enjoyed good health. He had excellent stamina on the basketball court. He never had a serious illness or injury. However, during his sophomore year, he began to have symptoms that worried both him and his mother. He noticed that he felt lightheaded during a basketball game. He became concerned that he might faint, because the feeling worsened as the game progressed.

He did not tell his coach and managed to get through the game. After the game, he told his parents. His father told him it was not a big deal and stated that James was just tired. Alice was more concerned. She asked James several questions. "Has this happened before? Do you get headaches? Do you feel nauseous? Did you bang your head?" Alice told James to go to bed early. She told him that if he did not feel well in the morning, she would call the doctor.

James got up the next morning and went down to breakfast. Alice was waiting for him when he got downstairs. "Are you still dizzy? Do you feel lightheaded?"

"I'm okay, Mom."

"I'm so relieved," Alice said. "I guess you were just tired."

Later that morning, Alice received a call from the school. She was told that James was not feeling well and had asked to be dismissed. Alice immediately drove to pick him up. "Is it happening again?" Alice asked.

"Yeah. But worse," James replied. "I kind of have a headache. I have an upset stomach too. I thought I was going to pass out in math class."

"Oh, James!" Alice exclaimed. "We are going right to the doctor's office."

The doctor examined James and found nothing obviously wrong. "He may be coming down with something," the doctor said. "He's probably just a bit run-down."

Over the next several days, James continued to have symptoms. He would feel fine, then without warning, he would get lightheaded and feel sick. He missed a couple of days of school and was dismissed early for the second time. Alice was frantic. She insisted that the doctor see him again. The result was the same. There was no apparent cause of James's problems.

As time passed, the situation worsened. James was getting headaches. He felt sick much of the day. He stopped participating in basketball practice and had a doctor's note excusing him "for medical reasons." Even Mike was worried. Alice had confided her worst fears to her husband. Then, one night, James expressed the same fear to them. James was not able to sleep. He was agitated and felt weak. His heart was racing. His head felt like it was under pressure. He had never felt like this before. He was terrified.

"Mom, I'm really sick," James said. "I don't know what's happening. I think I may be dying!"

"Mike, call an ambulance," Alice cried. "What is it, James? What's wrong?"

"I think I must have a brain tumor," James said.

This was exactly what Alice feared. James was crying. "Maybe it's my heart. I don't know. But something's wrong. I can tell. I'm having trouble breathing."

The ambulance came and James was seen at the emergency room. Four hours later, the doctors gave their diagnosis. James had a panic attack. His heart was fine. His brain was fine. He was having severe panic attacks. He was cleared medically and sent home. James was embarrassed, but relieved. His parents were exhausted but still frightened.

Alice and Mike came to see me to learn how to help James with his panic. When James heard about adrenaline and how it affected his body, he was greatly relieved. Adrenaline explained all of his physical symptoms. Adrenaline caused his lightheadedness, stomach distress, and racing heart. It also made him afraid and want to run, which is what he felt at school. He also felt relieved to know that many people feel like they are dying or having a nervous breakdown when they have a strong adrenaline response.

James and his parents learned about the biological basis for his symptoms. They began to talk about which thoughts made him release adrenaline. It was clear what set off this sequence. When James did not feel well, he began to speculate about what might be wrong. The first time he felt this way, he had worried he might faint during the game and embarrass himself. The next day these thoughts had continued, but were mixed with vague thoughts that maybe he was sick. When his symptoms did not go away, he began to wonder if he had a serious problem. That is when the idea that he might have a brain tumor or heart problem occurred to him. Once he began to have these thoughts, his adrenaline response went into high gear. He was afraid he was going to die.

Each time he had thoughts of brain tumors and death, he released a surge of adrenaline. This brought on the very symptoms that made him fearful. The physical sensations in his body only made his fears seem more real.

James was a very bright and motivated young man. He quickly understood the connection between his thoughts and his panic. He began to learn to control and change his thinking so that he could regulate his adrenaline. Over several weeks he gradually began to feel in control of his mind and body.

Alice was proud of her son and relieved he was not seriously ill. However, she also felt something else: guilt. She knew that her fears had been transferred to her son. Over the years, she had communicated her fears by worrying out loud and by repeated reminders for James to take precautions. She loved him dearly. The thought of losing him was more than she could bear. It helped her anxiety when she brought James to the doctor, even if her son was not sick. While she was reassured by these visits, she had taught James to worry like she did.

Alice decided to talk to James about her feelings. She wanted to modify the message she was giving him. She told him she wished she could have handled her anxieties differently while he was growing up. She told him that she wanted him to always be responsible about his health. However, she felt she had taught him to be overly preoccupied with it. She said she would try to help him find a better balance between being health conscious and overly preoccupied. She told him that she might need his help and feedback when she let her anxieties get out of control.

James understood his mother's confession. He told her that he understood she was showing her love through her concern for his safety. "We both have to stop worrying about me, Mom," he said. "We'll help each other."

You can teach your child to control his fears. Help him to see the connection between his thinking and his anxiety. Make the same changes in your own thinking. Don't let your fears spill over to your child. Model a style that will teach your child to cope with any challenge.

Key Points to Remember

❖ Children's fears change with development.

❖ Children often learn fears from their parents.

❖ Adrenaline causes the physical signs of anxiety.

❖ Adrenaline can be controlled by regulating thinking.

Chapter 11

Teasing

"I hate Kenny Johnson," Mark said as he walked in the door.

"What happened today?" his mother, Brenda, asked. "Did he tease you again?"

"Yeah, and I'm sick of it." Mark was 10 years old and in the fifth grade. He had complained several times about Kenny.

"Did you tell the teacher like I told you to do?" Brenda asked.

"Yes, I did. She said she didn't see him do it, so she couldn't do anything." Mark was on the verge of screaming and crying. "The other kids just laughed at me. They knew I told the teacher. They called me a baby and a tattletale."

"I know how hard this is for you, Mark. I am proud of you for not acting like Kenny." Brenda was glad her son was not cruel to other children, but her heart was breaking. She knew how much this teasing hurt him. He was a sensitive child; he felt these unkind words deeply.

"Kenny said that I was a geek-loser," Mark continued. "Then, he dumped my books on the ground. All the kids were watching and laughing."

"Oh, Mark, I'm sorry. What did you do?" his mother asked.

"I tried to do what you told me. I tried to ignore him," Mark explained. "But he wouldn't stop. The other kids kept laughing. Finally, I couldn't take it anymore, and I yelled back that I was going to tell the teacher.

"Mom, this ignoring thing isn't working," Mark complained. "Dad said I could hit somebody who was hurting me. I'm going to punch him in the face next time."

Mark's father, Dave, had not exactly said this to his son. Dave meant that Mark could fight back if another child hit him first. However, she knew that her husband actually did want Mark to slug Kenny. Dave thought this was the only way to stop the teasing. Dave was not a violent man. He was, however, furious after seeing his son tormented day after day. Brenda had to admit that she was running out of ideas but was against violence under any circumstances.

Mark had told his teacher about the teasing on several occasions. Brenda had called the teacher herself and had gotten nowhere. The teacher said that all the children tease, and she could not intervene every time a child complained. She said her policy was to intervene whenever she saw the teasing happen. Otherwise, it was up to the children to work out these disputes.

Brenda felt helpless. The school was not protecting her son. Her husband was ready to go after Kenny himself if the teasing did not stop. Her advice to Mark had always been to ignore teasing. This was the same advice she got from friends and Mark's pediatrician. Ignore it.

"Mom, can I go to a different school?" Mark asked. "I can't take this anymore. Everyday they tease and laugh at me. You have to do something. Can I go to school somewhere else?"

"Sweetheart, this must be so terrible for you," Brenda said. She did think it might be time to send him to a more supportive environment. There was a nice parochial school in town. She did not want Mark to run away from his problems, but felt he was being damaged by the abuse from his peers. "I'll talk to your father when he gets home about you possibly switching to St. Stephen's."

"Okay," Mark seemed relieved. "I'd rather go to reform school than go back to my school. But what should I do tomorrow?"

"Just ignore Kenny," Brenda sighed. She felt dishonest giving this advice. She knew it was not going to work. "Just ignore them all, honey."

Children can be cruel. For all of their innocence, children often hurt other children, and the damage can be serious. Some children are scarred by this cruelty, and the hurt remains long after the teasing stops. Many adults look back at their childhood and vividly remember the pain of being teased.

Unfortunately, many parents and educators do not effectively protect children from teasing. There are two reasons why these adults fail to adequately respond to these beleaguered children. The first reason is that many adults underestimate the damage caused by teasing. These parents and teachers dismiss the complaints and tears of the teased child, seeing him as overly sensitive. They see teasing as normal behavior and believe that all kids need to learn to cope with good-natured ribbing. These parents and teachers don't recognize that there can be a lasting, negative impact on the teased child's self-esteem and emotional adjustment. Sadly, some of these adults even tease children themselves. They see this as a mild form of reprimand or necessary feedback to their children.

The second reason adults do not respond actively to teasing is that they don't know what to do about it. The universal advice given to teased children is to ignore the insults. Most of the time, this recommendation does not work. Ignoring usually has little impact on teasing for reasons that will be explained shortly. Ignoring can even be detrimental. It is a passive approach that forces the teased child to helplessly endure the punishment in the hopes it will stop. Passivity is an ineffective strategy. Therapeutic Parenting supports active problem solving. It's important that the solutions you create with your child give him an active method for responding to teasing.

Why Ignoring Doesn't Work

Let's examine the dynamics behind teasing and why ignoring is ineffective. You will need to explain this process to your child. Ignoring is based on the principle that teasing will either stop or continue based on the reaction of the teased child. If the teased child responds by crying, tattling, or complaining, the bully gets the attention he seeks. When this happens, the teasing will continue. On the other hand, according to this theory, if the teasing is ignored, the bully gets no attention and the teasing will stop. If the teased child can endure the suffering, eventually the bully will give up since he is not getting the desired reaction from his victim.

Unfortunately, this theory does not adequately describe the forces that maintain teasing. The reaction of the teased child does play a role in the continuation of teasing. However, it is only a small part of the process. There are two more important variables that maintain teasing that have little to do with the reaction of the victim.

The first variable is the reaction of peers who witness the act. Teasing most often occurs with other children observing and even participating. Even if the teased child ignores the bully, these bystanders are not ignoring him. Instead, the onlookers are probably laughing and joking and patting the bully on the back for his biting sarcasm and witty put-downs. Most of the attention that the bully receives comes from these peers. No matter how well the teased child ignores the teasing, the bully is getting plenty of reinforcement. If, in a perfect world, these onlookers would also ignore the bully, then ignoring really would be a successful strategy. Some sophisticated teachers insist that all of their students ignore teasing. This is a more effective and supportive approach.

The second reason that ignoring does not work has to do with how the bully feels about herself. If her self-esteem is enhanced by diminishing another child, the bully will continue to tease. Unfortunately, many children do feel better about themselves when they make another child feel less powerful and less capable. Most bullies actually have low self-esteem and are insecure. They feel better about themselves when they feel strong and dominant. When they tease another child who is made to feel and appear weak, the bully feels more powerful and less insecure.

Unfortunately, "trash talking," put-downs, and intimidation are ingrained in our culture, especially for boys. These insults are viewed as cool, funny, and part of being manly. Our children are inundated with inappropriate role models on television and within sports. Athletes and professional wrestlers have perfected this form of aggressive verbal dominance. Much of the teasing perpetrated against defenseless children is learned, word for word, from these television shows and sports figures. When a bully mimics these antics and succeeds in dominating and hurting a sensitive child who is too well behaved to retaliate, the bully feels empowered by his "victory."

This victorious feeling for the bully is an internal state that does not necessary require external validation. If the bully believes he has "won" the exchange and feels better about himself, he will continue to tease even if he is ignored. Once again, this exposes the limitations of ignoring as a strategy.

Here is a sample monologue to explain these dynamics to your child:

"I know how awful it is to be teased. I am so proud of you for not being a bully and teasing other kids. I want you to understand why this boy teases you. It's not because there is anything wrong with you. You are wonderful. I know it feels like the other kids are laughing at you. Actually, they are trying to feel better about themselves. Some kids feel so badly about who they are that they'll try anything to feel better. If a bully can make you feel weak or sad, he will think he's strong and cool. Of course, teasing doesn't actually make him strong or cool. He is tricking himself into believing he is tough. The other kids laugh when he does this because they want the bully to think they like him, and because they don't want him to tease them. It's very wrong that this is happening to you. I want you to understand that this kid is teasing you because he wants to feel good about himself. This is not about you being a bad kid. The opposite is true. By not being like him, you prove what a good person you are."

Part of the solution for your child is to help her view the teasing differently. Teased children take the unkind words to heart and worry that what is being said about them is true. They also see the bully as in control and dominant. This monologue puts a more accurate perspective on the teasing. It confirms that you see your child as wonderful and that you are proud of him. The monologue also helps her to see the teaser differently. You are pointing out that the bully is acting out of weakness and insecurity. This realization allows your child to feel more empowered and less vulnerable.

Coping Strategies

In addition to restructuring your child's view of the bully, you will need to teach him new strategies. The goal behind this approach is to provide your child with an active response to teasing that undermines the dynamics that support the bully. Remember that Therapeutic Parenting is based on values. As you develop what you want your child to say and do, make sure that your strategy conforms to your values and teaches your child what you want him to learn.

Since your child is not going to ignore the teasing, she will have to say something. You will need to practice this with your child using TLC. Once you develop what your child will say, role-play the situation (see the following box). Let her be the bully, and you play the part of your child. Your job is to model what your child will say when she is teased. Then, switch roles. Keep practicing until your child feels comfortable.

Try a Role Play

After you develop a plan for how your child will respond to teasing, use a role play for practice:

- ❖ Start by having your child play the role of the bully, and you take the part of your child.

- ❖ Sensitively show him how he usually responds, so he can see how he looks to the bully.

- ❖ Then, do the role play again, but this time model the new way he is going to respond.

- ❖ Switch parts and let him play himself.

- ❖ Give him gentle, but necessary, feedback.

- ❖ Try to build up his confidence that he can carry out the plan.

- ❖ The next time he is teased, have him act out what happened in a new role play and then troubleshoot your plan.

- ❖ Make it fun!

Here are some ground rules for what your child can say in response to teasing:

- ❖ Her reply must conform to your values.
- ❖ She must not stoop to the level of the bully and tease back.
- ❖ She must feel empowered by her response.
- ❖ The bully and the bystanders must be surprised and confused about what to do in response to your child's new attitude.

The first set of options for you to consider stresses a wry, humorous approach to the teasing. This approach is particularly effective if your child is verbal and has a sense of humor. He may not be comfortable with this approach if he is overwhelmed with emotion when he is being teased. If the teasing makes him cry or he is overwhelmed with anger, he may not be ready for the subtlety of this first suggestion. On the other hand, if he has control over his emotions and likes the idea of using clever banter, he will feel comfortable with this idea.

This first approach requires your child to provide commentary on the teasing. In using this strategy, her tactic is to be a critic of the quality of the teasing. Her job is to respond to the teasing with evaluation and feedback as to how good it is and whether the bully should be satisfied with his efforts. This is meant to be a tongue-in-cheek reaction that relies on understated sarcasm. Here are some examples:

"That was the same line you used on me yesterday. Let's try to be a little more creative here."

"You need to work on your delivery. You're just going through the motions. Put a little heart into it."

"Hey, I liked that one. You're finally showing some creativity. Way to go! Let's have more of those."

"Did you think that was your best effort? It's not for me to decide about your performance, but I think that was pretty weak."

"I'm starting to really appreciate you. You have a real caring side that shows when you get like this. I can see it in your face."

Not all children can pull this off. When they can, these responses are highly effective. They will make your child seem amused by the teasing and impervious to the pain. These comments will also frustrate the teaser. His performance is being critiqued in this clever way. The bully will not get what he seeks from this response. He will not feel stronger or wittier. He will not get the reaction he wants from peers, who will be confused by your child's reactions.

Tell your child that the bully may react to any new strategy with an intensification of the teasing. There is a slight risk that a frustrated bully may become more aggressive. If this happens, you may need to contact a teacher to make sure your child is safe. Usually, however, these strategies don't elicit aggression. Instead, most bullies respond to these techniques with more name calling. Explain to your child that this is actually a good sign. It means that the teaser does not like your child's reaction and feels threatened and insecure. Your child should respond to this intensified teasing using the same approach:

"Now that's more like it! You are showing some real sincerity now."

"I can see you're trying harder. That's a good effort. Keep it up."

"Excellent! That was a really good one. Way to go, my man!"

These responses are actually quite sophisticated given what they do to the bully—they disempower her. She fails in her attempt to exert her dominance. She also does not look cool to peers who are watching the exchange. These are positive changes that will make your child feel like he has withstood the onslaught with his dignity intact.

There are variations on this approach. Some children don't feel comfortable with sarcasm. Teach your child other comebacks that may serve the same purpose. For example, your child can use creative vocabulary:

"That was egregious."

"My, you seem rambunctious today."

"Absolutely scintillating!"

These responses will be puzzling, as the bully's vocabulary may not include these words. Your child may like the look of bewilderment as the bully tries to figure out whether he has been insulted or complimented. The key to these techniques is to give your child an active option that doesn't leave him feeling conquered and demeaned. As long as the bully is uneasy, and he has not clearly dominated the situation, the interaction will be a success. In other words, a stalemate or draw is an acceptable outcome to break the pattern of teasing.

Some children are highly sensitive and have trouble using sarcasm and witty commentary. When children cry or get highly emotional while being teased, they need a different strategy. Sadly, bullies feel empowered when they cause another child to cry. If the teaser sees tears, she knows she has defeated her victim. This is one of the reasons that teasing is so cruel. Rather than eliciting sympathy, crying or distress usually leads to more taunting and shaming of the victim. This is yet another reason why ignoring does not work. If a child is crying or outwardly distressed, even if he does not say a word, he is communicating that the teasing has hit a nerve. The bully can tell that she has successfully dominated the distraught child.

If your child cries or is overtly upset, he will not feel genuine trying to appear bemused in the face of teasing. He will need to use another strategy. The key to this next approach is to put the bully on the spot about his cruelty. Rather than feeling strong and cool in front of his peers, the goal of this technique is to make the bully feel ashamed and embarrassed.

In this approach, the idea is to call attention to the process of what the bully is doing and why he is doing it. This includes having your child admit her pain and acknowledge that the bully has been successful. This is the opposite of keeping a stiff upper lip or ignoring the teasing. Rather, this strategy accentuates how much it hurts to be teased. Here are some examples of how your child can respond:

"Okay. You win. That really hurt me. I guess that's what you want. Congratulations, you've succeeded."

"Well, here I am crying. You've done it again. You've managed to make me feel awful and embarrassed in front of my friends."

"If you're trying to make me feel bad about myself, you've done a great job. I feel really hurt. Actually, I feel like a real jerk. I guess that's what teasing is supposed to do."

These comments are a setup for the second phase of this technique. The goal of this first set of statements is to highlight the pain your child is feeling. He does not have to fight to stay in control of his emotions. Instead, he uses his pain as a weapon. He flaunts the reality that he hurts, feels ashamed in front of his friends, and negatively about himself. He makes it unmistakably clear that these feelings are induced by the bully. He admits the success of the teasing.

The second phase of this technique is to question the motivation of the bully. The key is to make the bully, and anyone else observing, wonder why the bully would want to hurt someone else. These comments will raise questions about the bully. Remember that bullies tease to feel better about themselves and to impress their friends. To undermine this process, here is what your child can say:

"Do you feel good now? You can see how upset I am. What is it about hurting me so badly that makes you feel good?"

"Do you feel cool when I cry? Is that why you want to do this to me? When I'm crying, you seem so pleased with yourself. Why does this make you so happy?"

"You've managed to embarrass me in front of the whole class. Everyone is laughing at me. Do you feel really special when the other kids see you do this? Will you do anything to be the center of attention even if it really hurts someone else? Why is it so important to you to have kids laugh at what you say?"

"You know, I actually feel bad for you. You must really be hurting inside. It's the only reason I can think of for why you want to hurt me this way. If hurting me makes you feel better about yourself, you must be pretty messed up."

These are heavy-hitting comments. They shine a bright light on the motivation of the bully. Her actions have been redefined. She is not cool, funny, or strong. Rather, she is cruel, insecure, and desperate for attention. Your child's tears and pain confirm this reality. Now, instead of your child seeming weak and defenseless, she will appear noble. She will have taken the moral high ground. She acknowledges how much she hurts but refuses to retaliate using the bully's tactics.

Remind your child that this strategy also has the potential to lead to a temporary escalation of the teasing. The kind of escalation resulting from this strategy is actually somewhat predictable. Here are the kinds of things bullies invariably say in response to this technique:

"Yeah, I like to make you hurt because you're such a loser."

"I feel great when I see you cry. I love making babies cry."

The bully will never admit his shame or weakness when your child confronts him. Instead, he will act as if he is pleased with what he has done. Prepare your child for this kind of reaction. Your child should respond by keeping up the same kinds of comments:

"Then, I guess you're getting what you want, because it sure does hurt."

"I don't understand why this makes you so happy. What's so cool about hurting someone else?"

These comments perpetuate the same theme. They keep the focus on the bully, her cruelty, and the satisfaction she derives. Some bullies actually do have a conscience and will feel guilty. Others will not feel guilt but will not like how they appear to their friends. Either way, this approach will make things better.

Practice this technique with your child. At first, he may be uncomfortable. It takes courage and determination to confront a bully in this way. Empathize with your child that this is a challenge. He will be motivated because he will want the teasing to stop. He will also be glad to have an option that allows him to take action. Ignoring has only made him feel passive and powerless.

There are other techniques that may help your child. These ideas can be used in combination with the others:

❖ Have your child take a pencil and paper and write down exactly what the bully says. This will make the bully a bit paranoid about why your child is keeping this record. Your child can say, "Could you repeat that last line? I didn't quite get it all down. You said I was a dweeb-loser and then I missed the next part. What was it again?"

❖ Give ratings to the teasing. Your child can give his rating orally, or she can even hold up a card like a gymnastics judge at the Olympics. "That was a five. Not your best effort."

❖ Your child can address any onlookers and get them to evaluate the teasing. "What do the rest of you think? Is it just me, or is he slipping?" Or, "Do you guys see what I see? Doesn't he seem to love being cruel? What do you guys make of that?"

❖ Your child can go up to the bully and ask to be teased. "You haven't teased me yet today. I need to follow a routine. It's time. Come on, give it to me. I want it. Bring it on!"

❖ Your child can put an intentionally surprising label on the motivations of the bully. "I think you must really like me. There are better ways to try to get me to like you. The more you tease me, the more obvious it is that you're desperate for my attention. Admit it. You want me to pay attention to you, don't you?"

As you develop plans, be creative in finding a solution. Some highly effective strategies attack teasing indirectly by subtly influencing peer relationships or by enhancing your child's social standing. Here are some examples of these solutions:

❖ Have your child invite the bully to your home to play or to go to an activity together.

❖ Suggest your child run for class president, try out for the school play, or write for the school newspaper.

❖ Help your child develop new activities with a different group of children than the ones who tease him.

❖ Find a volunteer experience where your child can help others.

❖ Suggest she identify other children who are nice to her, who may also be getting teased, and pursue friendships with them.

❖ Enlist the assistance of teachers to help teach the values of being caring to classmates.

There is another level of solutions to consider that can help your child deal with teasing. This level is sensitive, so proceed with caution. Some children may say or do things that make them easy targets for teasing, or that provoke other children. If your child is doing some of these things that elicit teasing, examine her actions with her. If she is provoking teasing by doing something that does not conform to your family values or is socially immature, she should change her behavior. For example, your child may be teasing other children, then complaining when she is teased in return. Your child may seek attention by annoying others. She may lack the social skills to make friends. Help your child identify things she is doing that lead to teasing, and evaluate if she should change her actions.

The reason for caution is that you don't want him to feel bad about who he is or what he believes. Some things that make him stand out as a target might be things he should be proud of and that he should not change. If your son is teased because he likes to sing in a choir or act in plays, he should feel good about this and not change merely to avoid teasing. Some children are teased because they have skills and interests that don't conform to stereotypes. You should help your child feel good about these unique talents or activities.

Many children are teased because they don't conform to current trends. Others are teased because they don't listen to the "right" kind of music. Many children are teased based on how they dress. There is enormous peer pressure beginning at early ages to look and act the same. If your child does not conform, he is more likely to be a target. (For more, see Chapter 13, "Peer Pressure.")

When Should You Call the Teacher?

Children don't want to be tattletales. But sometimes parents have to call a teacher when teasing goes too far. When is it time for you to get involved? Make the call when your child ...

* ❖ Does not want to go to school because of teasing.
* ❖ Is avoiding most of his classmates while at school.
* ❖ Seems to be getting depressed.
* ❖ Has been injured by a bully.
* ❖ Is expressing violent fantasies of getting revenge.
* ❖ Tells you he needs your help.

If you've talked with your child's teacher and gotten no results, talk with the school principal.

Use TLC to discuss your values and expectations about these conformity issues. You may value your child's individuality in her pursuit of activities, interests, or appearance. However, her individuality may lead to painful teasing and peer pressure. What are the values you want to teach your child in these circumstances? Should she conform to avoid social ostracism? Or, should she keep acting differently at the expense of intense teasing? This is not an easy dilemma. Most parents seek a compromise solution that allows the child to be less of a target while not sacrificing his individuality.

Gino could really dance. He had started taking dance lessons when he was three. Now, at age 15, he had won many dance competitions, including some national awards. He had plans to be a professional dancer. At the dance studio, Gino was highly respected and well liked. Most of the other dancers were girls. There was only one other boy his age who took dancing at the same studio. Gino was acutely aware of the negative stereotypes that were associated with male dancers.

"Hey, Gino, where's your tutu?" Gino recognized the voice. It was Curt, the most vocal of his taunting classmates. "Why don't you pirouette into your seat, you faggot."

Gino ignored Curt's teasing, but the other students did not. Several of the boys in the class laughed at Curt's remark. One of them gave Curt a high five. Gino took his seat in class. He was so tired of all the teasing. It happened every day. He was laughed at and ridiculed because he danced, and everyone assumed he was gay. The teasing had been going on for months. Most boys at school would not hang around with him because they feared it would make them look gay.

The truth was that Gino was unsure whether or not he was gay. He knew that he danced because he loved to dance. He also knew that most of the time he disliked boys. He had so much resentment toward the boys who teased him that he couldn't imagine being attracted to one. However, after years of taunts and accusations about being gay, Gino was confused about his sexual identity.

His life seemed to be going in two irreconcilable directions. In school, he was feeling like an outcast. At the studio, he felt valued as a talented performer. He was not sure he could continue to withstand the strains of living in two different worlds.

Gino's mother, Mary, noticed that Gino had been distressed. She had tried to talk to her son, but he did not reveal much about how he felt. Gino's father had died when Gino was very young. Mary felt the need to be both mother and father to her son.

"Gino, what's the matter, sweetheart?" Mary asked. "You haven't eaten a thing. You seem upset. What is it?"

"It's nothing, Mom. I'm just not hungry." Gino smiled at his mother. He did not want to tell her what the boys were saying. He did not want to upset her. He was also embarrassed to tell her that the boys thought he was gay. However, Gino was running out of patience with the teasing. He didn't know what to do. Maybe he should fight with Curt and prove he wasn't gay. Maybe he should quit dancing. He was confused, but he was also feeling more desperate and alone.

The next day at school, Curt was waiting at Gino's locker. "Hey, Gino, I brought you a present. I wanted to make up with you." Curt held out a brown paper bag for Gino to take. Gino was leery. He knew it was a trick. Curt was not the kind of guy to buy him a present. Gino was also aware that several of Curt's friends were standing around watching.

"No thanks, Curt," Gino said as he refused to take the bag. "I don't want any of your presents."

"Oh, but you'll like this one," Curt said with a huge grin. Curt reached into the bag and took out a girl's dance costume, no doubt a relic from a little sister's dance recital. "It's perfect for you, Gino. Come on. Put it on and dance for us." Curt was laughing. The bystanders were laughing. Gino was furious. He was also close to tears. He walked away and left the building. He went home, hoping his mother had left for work. She was still home.

"Gino, what are you doing home?" Mary looked puzzled and worried. "Are you sick? Is everything okay?"

Gino began to cry. "Mom, I can't take it anymore. The boys at school tease me everyday about dancing. They all think I'm gay. I'm going to have to give up dancing. I can't deal with this anymore."

Mary was stunned. "Gino, dancing is such a big part of your life. I can't believe after all your work and success that you would give it up."

"I know, Mom. I haven't told you what I've been going through," Gino explained. "Every day the boys are on my case. They call me a fag. I try to ignore them, but they won't let up. Maybe if I quit dancing they'll leave me alone."

"I feel so bad that you have had to go through this," Mary replied. "I should have realized something was going on. Let's figure this out together."

Mary was a wonderful mother who was determined to help her son. Mary came to see me. She learned how to use TLC and how to generate new ideas to help Gino. She encouraged him to look at his options for dealing with the teasing. He was open to trying a new approach. However, he was nervous about how Curt would react to his new strategy. Gino knew that Curt would test him soon.

"Hey, Dancer the Prancer, worn any nice skirts lately?" It was a line that Curt had used before. The other boys still seemed to think it was funny, since they were snickering.

"Curt, my man, you haven't called me Dancer the Prancer in almost two weeks," Gino replied, trying to smile. *"I like when you make the extra effort to rhyme when you insult me. We all get to see your poetic side. See, we are really soul mates, after all. I'm a dancer; you're a poet."* The other boys giggled at this line. Curt did not.

"I'm not your soul mate, faggot," Curt hissed. I don't like girly boys." Curt had moved closer to Gino. It was an implied threat.

"Now, I really am hurt," Gino said, still trying to smile. *"I always thought your preoccupation with me was a sign you cared. Why else would you spend so much time paying attention to me?"* Gino's heart was really pounding, but he wasn't quite done. *"Come on, Curt. Don't be afraid of your feelings. You know you tease me because you care."* Gino thought he was going to faint while he watched Curt's face twist into a snarl.

The other boys were laughing harder now. This was a good show. *"I'm going to kick your butt, you little faggot, if you ever talk to me like this again,"* Curt said with fists clenched.

One of the boys started to laugh hysterically. *"Hey, Curt,"* the boy said, *"I think you should leave his butt alone. He might like that."*

All the other boys began to laugh. *"Yeah, you're right. I don't think I want to mess with a fag's butt,"* Curt said. He seemed relieved to have a way to save face and began to walk away.

"Wait a minute, Curt," Gino called after him. *"You're still going to call me names though, right? I mean, 'How am I supposed to live without you, after you've been loving me so long?'"*

The other boys laughed at this line. Curt turned and gave Gino the finger.

Mary was worried when she heard Gino's recounting of the story. She was afraid that Curt would attack her son. Gino told her that he could handle *himself. In fact, Gino was very athletic and powerful. "Mom, I did okay today," Gino said.*

"I'm proud of you, Gino," Mary said. "Just be careful."

Curt did try to tease Gino the next day. Gino thanked Curt and told him he was worried that Curt was going to stop paying attention to him. As the days passed, Curt just snarled and glared.

Gino made the decision to keep dancing. With his mother's encouragement, he also decided to make a bold move. The school's yearly variety show was coming up, and he decided to participate. He had not planned to do this, since he felt it would call attention to his dancing and increase the teasing. Gino was feeling stronger. He was a dancer, and proud of it.

Mary was very anxious as she sat in the audience waiting for her son to dance. She had watched him perform countless times before, but this was different. He was revealing himself to his peers, several of whom had ridiculed him for this very talent.

When his turn came, Gino danced with passion and great athleticism. The crowd began to respond. They clapped and cheered as he crossed the stage doing back flips. When he was finished, they stood and applauded. Mary was crying. The crowd was going wild. Few had realized until now that one of their fellow students was actually a nationally recognized dancer with exceptional talent.

Gino stood at center stage, bowed, then rose and pumped a clenched fist. He was going to be a hard act to follow.

Teasing is an act of cruelty. Your child will need your support in coping with the emotional pain inflicted by insensitive peers. Use TLC to discuss his feelings and create a plan. Help him develop an effective approach to counteract teasing. Teach him that action-oriented solutions are the best way to tackle adversity.

Key Points to Remember

❖ Ignoring teasing does not make it stop.

❖ Bullies tease because they are insecure and need peer validation.

❖ Your child will feel more in control with an action-oriented strategy.

❖ Use TLC to develop creative solutions to teasing.

Chapter 12

Self-Esteem

Shawn dreaded this nightly routine. It was time for his 11-year-old daughter, Molly, to do her homework. He and his daughter always ended up frustrated and tense.

"So, Molly, how's the homework coming along?" Shawn asked with as much cheer as he could muster.

"Bad," his daughter replied dejectedly.

"What's the problem?" Shawn asked, even though he knew the answer to his own question.

"I can't do this," Molly said. "I don't understand the problems. How can I do my homework if I don't know how to do it?"

"Molly, you say that every night, and then you figure it out," Shawn said with a hint of exasperation in his voice. "You are a very smart girl. You could get all As if you put your mind to it."

"I can't figure these problems out. You're the one who figures them out. I can't do math," Molly complained.

"Molly, I don't like that attitude," Shawn said sternly. His patience was worn thin from this nightly dialogue. "Your teacher says you are smart and that you understand the math. She said it's just a matter of self-confidence."

"She's wrong," Molly barked. "I'm stupid. All the other kids know it, too. I'm dumb, Dad. I can't do this. I can't do my reading assignment either. I don't know what topic to pick for my report."

Shawn was struggling to keep his emotions under control. This was so typical of Molly. His daughter always belittled herself, calling herself stupid or other insulting names. She acted helpless whenever she faced a challenge. Molly did not believe in her own abilities.

This self-deprecating attitude extended beyond schoolwork. Molly complained about her appearance. She also said that no one liked her, which was not true. When Molly played sports, she gave up at the first sign of adversity. Shawn was alarmed by this pervasive helplessness and low self-esteem. He wanted his daughter to persevere when facing a challenge and to believe in herself. Instead, Molly crumbled whenever she faced a difficult situation.

Molly knew that her father was disappointed in her. This only made things worse. When Shawn pushed Molly, they both ended up distressed. But what was Shawn supposed to do? He believed it was his responsibility as a father to push his daughter to achieve and persevere.

"Come on, Molly," Shawn said. "Let me see you try to solve this problem. I know you can do it."

"What is it about the word 'stupid' that you don't understand, Dad?" Molly replied. "I can't do this problem. I can't do anything! I'm just a loser."

"That's enough, Molly." Shawn was tired of these self-loathing soliloquies. "Either you get your homework done now, or you will not watch any TV tonight. I know you can do this, so stop acting like a helpless baby." Shawn regretted the words as soon as they came out of his mouth.

It's a common paradox that many competent, well-behaved children do not like themselves. Their low self-esteem is incongruous, since these children are often well liked and successful. These children reveal their feelings by making disparaging and insulting remarks about themselves. This is frustrating to parents who are aware of the inaccuracy of their children's self-perception. These parents see their children's abilities and positive qualities. Unfortunately, these children don't appreciate their own talents or take advantage of their opportunities.

Self-esteem begins to form early in childhood, as children gradually learn what pleases their parents and what doesn't. They realize that some behaviors meet with parental approval, while others lead to a negative response. This is the beginning of the development of self-esteem, as children evaluate themselves based on parental feedback.

The Roots of Self-Esteem

As children get older, they develop a more complete picture of who they are and whether they are valued and successful. They integrate the perspectives of siblings, peers, and teachers into their self-evaluations. They broaden the categories that make up self-esteem to include how they act, how they look, their popularity, and success in school and athletics. In addition, their self-esteem forms depending upon their personality traits, including whether they are outgoing or shy; take initiative or are passive; and whether they are caring or cold. Self-esteem is complex and hard to define since it is made up of so many specific elements.

Another factor that is confusing about self-esteem is that it can vary dramatically within the same child. Children are highly influenced by the immediacy of their lives. A child can feel poorly about himself one minute and then exude confidence shortly thereafter.

Low self-esteem is not a blatant behavior problem like aggression or tantrums. It is not an emotional problem like depression or anxiety. Rather, it is a state of mind that affects a child's confidence, effectiveness, and satisfaction.

When children have low self-esteem, it shows in a variety of ways. Here are some of the signs children display when they have low self-esteem:

❖ **Negative statements about themselves.** For example, these children may say, "I can't do anything right. I hate myself. I'm such a loser."

❖ **Lack of self-confidence.** These children are reluctant to try new things, and they act passively in unfamiliar circumstances.

❖ **Lack of perseverance.** Children with low self-esteem give up easily whenever they are faced with a challenge.

❖ **Difficulty accepting responsibility for their actions.** These children blame others when there is a problem and do not own up to their mistakes.

❖ **Constant need for reassurance.** Children with low self-esteem ask for positive feedback and cannot complete tasks without continuous guidance and praise for their efforts.

❖ **Anxiety in social situations.** These children feel inadequate relative to other children and worry about not being liked.

❖ **Frustration over lack of achievement.** When these children do not meet performance expectations academically or athletically, they demonstrate their frustration by being disagreeable or noncompliant.

On the other hand, children with high self-esteem show the opposite characteristics:

❖ **Perseverance and self-confidence.** These children are willing to try new things and are not afraid to fail. They expect to succeed and enjoy challenges.

❖ **Leadership.** Children with healthy self-esteem are natural leaders. They want to be in charge, and other children usually look up to them.

❖ **Responsibility for their actions.** When children feel good about themselves, they can accept their mistakes. They are willing to acknowledge what they did wrong and are open to feedback about how to improve.

❖ **Even temperament.** When children have positive self-esteem, they are less moody and are not easily frustrated. They tend to be pleasant and cooperative.

Your parenting style is not the only factor in the development of your child's self-esteem; it is merely the most important. Since low self-esteem is a broad and somewhat mysterious process, it's difficult for parents to know what to do about it. However, you can do a great deal to help your child feel good about herself.

Promoting Healthy Self-Esteem

Therapeutic Parenting stresses three core factors for parents to promote healthy self-esteem in their children. These factors are related to the key components of Therapeutic Parenting: validating your child, holding your child accountable for his actions, and teaching your child honest self-appraisal. Let's take a closer look at each of these factors.

Core Factor #1: Validate Your Child

Your child must always believe that you value, respect, and love her. Even when you are unhappy with something she does, she must never doubt your acceptance of her. You must make her feel that she is a wonderful child who is special.

If your child has doubts about how you feel, he will have low self-esteem. Believing that you value him is an absolute, necessary prerequisite to his positive self-esteem. Your validation does not guarantee he will feel good about himself. However, it is certain that he will develop a poor self-concept if he worries that you do not value him. After all, how could he be happy with himself if he were to believe that you were not happy with him?

Looking for Strengths

Children with low self-esteem have trouble seeing their positive qualities. Help your child to see his strengths by ...

❖ Telling her nice things people have told you about your child.

❖ Asking him to tell you one thing every day that he did well.

❖ Praising subtle qualities like sensitivity, meticulous workmanship, kindness to small children, or loyalty to friends.

❖ Requesting her help with a project or job.

❖ Asking for his opinions.

❖ Giving her an important responsibility.

❖ Developing his talents by enrolling in classes or activities in which he excels.

Don't confuse validating your child with giving her unconditional positive feedback. You need to teach your child values and let her know when she does something wrong. However, the way you give corrective feedback is critical. Your child must never be confused about how you feel about her, even when you are teaching her to learn from her mistakes.

Some parents damage their child's self-esteem by being overly harsh in pointing out a child's deficits. They may make disparaging remarks about their child when giving corrective feedback. Or the tone of the feedback may be so hostile that the child feels invalidated. Parents make these mistakes out of frustration and worry. They are trying to encourage their child to be more responsible, hardworking, or willing to accept challenges. Although these parents are trying to help, a harsh style can create a bigger problem.

Here's an example of this damaging scenario. Let's say a parent is frustrated and worried over his child's lack of effort in school. The parent wants the child to try harder and achieve at a level consistent with her ability. The parent, worried about his daughter's future, overreacts and says, "Mary, I think you are just plain lazy. I am so disappointed in you. I have tried to teach you the value of hard work, but you won't learn. What's the matter with you? You'll never amount to anything the way you are going. Mark my words. You'll end up cooking hamburgers the rest of your life. I see it coming. You just don't care. I give up. I am tired of wasting my time on you."

This feedback is highly invalidating. It sounds as if the parent is so disappointed that he sees no hope for the child. This message will not lead to greater achievement. Rather, it will convince the child that she is a bad person who is unworthy of her parent's love and respect. Over time, this form of feedback undermines the relationship between parent and child and ravages the child's view of herself.

Here are some of the common mistakes you must avoid to protect your child's self-esteem:

- ❖ **Insulting and demeaning comments.** Don't call your child names, tease him, or defame his character.

- ❖ **Being overly critical.** Pick your battles and don't correct or punish every misdeed.

- ❖ **Using a harsh, angry tone.** A condescending or hostile style of communication can be even more hurtful than the words themselves.

- ❖ **Inducing excessive guilt.** Don't burden your child with the perception that what she has done wrong is a horrible misdeed. In particular, don't overstate the damage done to you from his mistakes: "You have ruined my life!"

- ❖ **Never being satisfied.** If his best is never good enough, he will always feel he has disappointed you.

- ❖ **Reminding her of her failures.** Do not continuously remind her of past mistakes in the hope it will help her correct her performance.

- ❖ **Telling him he is hopeless.** Never make him feel it is too late to change and make his life better.

It's important that you examine your actions carefully and honestly. Make sure your feedback about helping her learn from mistakes does not cross the line. Correct your child in a way that protects your relationship and supports her self-esteem. Here are some guidelines to follow when giving her feedback:

- ❖ **Focus on positive behavior.** Strengthen his positive behavior by giving him lots of praise and support when he does the right things.

- ❖ **Be respectful.** Always give feedback in a way that protects her dignity and models how you want her to speak to you.

- ❖ **Focus on his actions.** When giving negative feedback, describe the problem with his behavior. Do not tell him that *he* is the problem.

- ❖ **Emphasize your values.** Clarify your family values and expect that she follow them.

- ❖ **Validate him as a person.** Especially when giving negative feedback, preface your comments with praise for the kind of person he is and the faith you have in him.

The following monologue demonstrates how to give negative feedback while still validating your child:

> "Josh, you know how much I believe in you and love you. I think you're a wonderful son. But something is bothering me about how you've been treating your sister. I know you believe in being caring, but you've been unkind to her. You call her names and tease her. I expect you to do the right thing and start treating her with more sensitivity."

This feedback is respectful and stresses values. It models a style of feedback you want your child to emulate. The message validates him as a person, while identifying the problems with his behavior.

Core Factor #2: Hold Your Child Accountable for His Actions

Helping your child develop positive self-esteem includes teaching him to be accountable and responsible. While the first core factor stressed how to validate your child, the second factor deals with ensuring that he learns to do the right things for himself and others.

Some parents are positive and praising, yet their children have low self-esteem. It is not enough to be caring and sensitive as a parent to ensure a child will feel good about herself. Children have responsibilities and expectations to meet. As they grow older, children have an increasing awareness of what it takes to be successful. They also learn what it means to be a good person. When children fail to meet these expectations, they don't feel good about themselves. These expectations include the following:

- ❖ Treating others respectfully
- ❖ Achieving in school
- ❖ Helping around the house
- ❖ Adhering to family values
- ❖ Taking care of one's personal hygiene
- ❖ Learning to function independently
- ❖ Learning to protect one's safety

It is your responsibility to help your child learn to do these things. For him to succeed, you must hold him accountable to develop good habits and skills. Some parents are not consistent in supporting children while they learn to do these things. When children do not develop these skills, they remain overly dependent on parents. They cannot accomplish developmentally appropriate tasks without a lot of help. These children constantly need their parents to remind them to do chores, sit with them while they do homework, and punish them when they don't act correctly. In short, these children fail at the job of being successful.

Children need to develop competencies in order to have good self-esteem. When children are unable to meet their responsibilities, they feel inadequate. They are not respected by teachers and peers, and they frustrate their parents by being overly dependent.

Your challenge is to teach your child this accountability and to expect her to meet her responsibilities. You must, however, continue to validate her and be caring. Finding this balance is difficult. If you err too far in either direction, her self-esteem will be affected. If you are too demanding of her performance and critical of her mistakes, she will feel criticized and invalidated. If you are too lax in expecting her to meet her responsibilities, she will not learn accountability and will not develop competencies. It is crucial to find the right zone between these two extremes.

Here are some ways parents drift off course in holding their children accountable for their actions:

- **Low expectations.** These parents expect little from their children. They don't insist on good performance in school or at home. They are satisfied with whatever their children do or achieve.

- **Unrealistically high expectations.** These parents expect too much of their children. The expectations are so high that they are often unattainable. Their children are held accountable to a standard that makes them feel like perpetual failures.

- **False praise.** Some parents give such inflated praise or feedback that it is not genuine. These parents blame others for their children's mistakes. They do not give accurate, corrective feedback to help their children grow.

❖ **Inconsistent feedback.** Some parents know what they expect of their children but are inconsistent in their feedback. It's demanding for parents to hold children accountable. Sometimes it's easier for parents to "do it themselves." This inconsistent response interferes with children learning responsibility.

❖ **Reliance on punishment.** Sometimes children need punishment to back up a value or to correct a serious mistake. However, some parents rely too heavily on punishment to teach accountability.

The expectations you establish must be age appropriate, consistent, and value based. When your child does not meet these expectations, hold him accountable by giving feedback, redirection, encouragement, and suggestions for how to be successful. At times, you will also need to set limits or punish him for his transgressions.

Here is an example of a monologue for how to discuss expectations with a child who has been lying:

"I think you are a very capable and talented kid. I am so proud of you for the kind of person you are. But I also think you haven't been as honest as I expect you to be. Being honest is how people learn to trust each other. This is a very important value to me, and I know you want to be more honest. From now on, I want you to think before you say anything that's not true. Catch yourself before you speak and remind yourself how important it is to tell the truth. I expect this kind of honesty from you. Let's give this a try."

Without a set of expectations, your child will not achieve and will not be independent. She needs your help in developing a standard for her actions. By holding her accountable, you will teach her a work ethic and a values-based lifestyle.

Core Factor #3: Teach Your Child Honest Self-Appraisal

Your feedback and redirection are necessary, but temporary, supports to help your child meet his responsibilities. He needs to learn to monitor his own performance and to give himself corrective feedback. When he has done well, he deserves to recognize his success and feel good about himself. When he has failed to meet his own expectations, he needs to realize his deficiency and figure out what he is going to do to fix the problem.

The key to successful self-appraisal is honesty and accuracy. Honest self-appraisal can be painful. Many people avoid dealing with their shortcomings because it's difficult to accept the reality of their mistakes and failures. Avoidance is a common problem in people with low self-esteem. These individuals rationalize their behavior and avoid taking responsibility for it. There are many ways to use mental gymnastics to twist out of holding oneself accountable. In the short run, this avoidance is comforting. Over time, however, avoiding the truth about one's mistakes or problems undermines self-esteem.

Surprisingly, people who are the most honest about their shortcomings, and who are willing to take action to fix their mistakes, have the highest self-esteem. The paradox is that honest self-awareness of one's deficits does not lower self-esteem. Rather, accurate self-appraisal, followed by action to correct the deficit, raises self-esteem.

Teach your child to evaluate herself honestly. Show her that dealing with the truth about herself is always better. If she evaluates herself honestly and likes what she has done, she can feel good about her accomplishments. If her evaluation shows that she has not done the right thing, she will be unhappy with her performance. However, she will feel good about herself for being truthful. She will know that she needs to correct her mistake. Either way, your child will know that her self-evaluation is genuine and honest. This is how self-respect develops. By not avoiding the truth or running away from problems, she will begin to see herself as a person who tackles issues head-on.

How to Give Negative Feedback

Here are techniques for how to give your child negative feedback without damaging his or her self-esteem:

* Before you give negative feedback, mention two or three positive qualities. For example, "You've been doing a good job on your tests in school, and I can see how hard you study, but you still rush through your homework assignments."

* Never criticize a child's qualities, only his behavior. "I know you're a sensitive person, but that comment hurt your sister's feelings."

* Tell your child you are giving this feedback because you believe in her. "I know you can be successful, that is why I believe you are giving up too easily."

* Remind him that since you give negative feedback, it means he can trust your positive comments. "I tell you the truth, which includes pointing out something you did wrong. When I tell you what I admire about you, it is not fake praise. It is what I truly believe about you."

You will have many opportunities to help your child develop the value of honest self-appraisal. Whenever you give her positive or negative feedback, don't simply tell her your evaluation. Ask her how she evaluates her own actions. Prompt her to reflect on her own behavior. Does she feel good about what she has done? Is she proud of herself? Should she have done something differently?

Compare his self-appraisal to your perspective. Discuss discrepancies in a respectful manner. Help him to develop accurate self-awareness. Some children are overly critical of themselves. When you notice this, explain to your child how you think he is off base. You don't want him to be negative or down on himself. You want him to be accurate. This includes giving himself credit when he deserves it. Show him the right balance by comparing your evaluation to his and discussing the differences. When he is too easy on himself or avoids looking at his mistakes, gently assist him in seeing what he has missed. Praise him for his willingness to admit his mistakes. Teach him to be active in making plans to correct his deficits. Use TLC to develop strategies to make changes.

Here is an example of how this may play out between you and your child. Let's say that your child brings home her report card, and you believe it reflects insufficient effort. While your corrective feedback is important, it is even more critical that your child evaluate herself accurately. When you discuss this with her, ask her what she thinks about her grades. Is she satisfied? Does she think she worked as hard as she should have? Does she plan to do anything differently next term?

If your child sees his effort as insufficient, let him know that you are proud of his honest self-appraisal. Tell him you respect his mature perspective and his willingness to recognize what he needs to do to improve. Offer your assistance and develop a plan.

However, if your child says that she is pleased with her performance, you need to discuss the difference in your perspectives. It may be that your perspective is distorted, and you have unrealistically high expectations of your child's performance. Use honest self-appraisal in evaluating your expectations. Listen with an open mind to your child's point of view and be prepared to correct your expectations if you have been unreasonable. If, on the other hand, you still think your child is avoiding her responsibilities, you need to point this out.

Here is how you could deliver this message:

"I understand that you think you worked hard in school this term. Your opinion is important to me. I think it's even more important how you see yourself. Sometimes, being honest means admitting to yourself that you are not satisfied with something you have done. Never be afraid to tell yourself the truth. Now, my opinion is that you should have worked harder in school this term. I think you should put in more effort next term. I hope you will, at least, look carefully at how hard you are working. I want you to make sure that you are honest with yourself and that you are not avoiding your responsibilities. I believe in you and know that you will do the right thing."

By focusing on the three core factors of self-esteem, you will help your child develop a positive view of himself. Remember that he does not have to be extraordinarily successful in his accomplishments to have good self-esteem. Rather, he needs to know that you are proud of him. He needs to be held accountable for his actions and learn honest and accurate self-appraisal.

Appraising Your Performance As a Parent

Your self-esteem is related to these same core factors. As a parent, you must hold yourself accountable for how you meet your responsibilities, including how you raise your child. Honest self-appraisal of your parenting is critical. Don't avoid examining your performance. Don't be afraid of recognizing your faults as a parent. If you know in your heart that you should be doing a better job, confront this reality directly. Admit your deficits. Find new solutions and try them out. Your self-esteem will rise when you commit to this process. Your validation will come both from how you view yourself and from the changes you see in your child.

"This looks awful, Mom," Sandy said as she looked in the mirror. This was the fourth dress she had tried on during this shopping trip. Sandy was going to her first semiformal dance in three weeks. She was finishing her sophomore year in high school and had been invited to go to the dance by a boy in the

197

junior class. Sandy was initially very excited, but finding a dress she liked was quite an ordeal for her and her mother, Linda.

"All of the dresses look great on you, honey," Linda said. "I like them all."

"What are you talking about?" Sandy hissed. "I'm so fat, it is disgusting."

"Sweetheart, you're not fat. You're beautiful," Linda said trying to remain calm. She was getting frustrated and tense from her daughter's reactions.

"Mother, I am trying on a size 12," Sandy snapped. "And, some of those are too small. I am gross, Mom. I can't believe anyone even asked me to the dance. I wish I wasn't going. I can't stand looking in the mirror for another minute."

"Well, I think you are perfect," Linda replied. "Any boy who takes you to the dance is lucky. Maybe we should take a break from shopping, though. This is getting too unpleasant."

"Mother, I need a dress," Sandy barked. "I am fat. Fat! I'll never find a dress." They agreed to go to one more store. The results were the same.

As they drove home, Linda did not know what to say or do for her daughter. Sandy was a wonderful girl. She was popular, caring to others, and a good student. Linda was concerned because Sandy had been saying such terrible things about herself. She even thought that no one liked her. This was not true. Sandy was popular and had many friends.

Linda tried to be consistently positive toward her daughter. She never said anything negative. The truth was that Sandy was overweight. However, Linda was in a bind. She did not want her daughter to be one of those girls who was preoccupied with weight and who developed an eating disorder. Linda was determined to make her daughter feel good about herself no matter how much she weighed. She felt if she acknowledged that Sandy was overweight, it would confirm Sandy's worst fear. Linda was confused, and her daughter was unhappy with herself.

Linda also knew in her heart that there was a reason for Sandy's weight issue. Her daughter did not take care of her health through exercise or good eating habits. She did not participate in sports or active recreational activities. She loved junk food. She was not living a healthy lifestyle. However, how could Linda address these issues without making Sandy feel that she was fat and unattractive?

Now that she saw how badly Sandy felt about herself, Linda wondered if she had made a mistake in being too accepting of her daughter's bad habits. Linda had always let Sandy regulate what she ate and whether she participated in sports. Perhaps, Linda thought, she should have played a more active role in encouraging her daughter to take care of herself. Linda had never given Sandy feedback about the repercussions of her lifestyle.

Linda felt she had contributed to Sandy's low self-esteem. She felt guilty for cooperating by buying the junk food that Sandy had requested. She should have expected her daughter to adhere to a more disciplined lifestyle. It was difficult for Linda to admit the truth about her mistakes, but she knew it was true. She realized she needed to correct her approach.

When they arrived home, Sandy went right to her room. A short time later, Linda heard crying. She knocked on Sandy's door and asked if they could talk. "Tell me what you're feeling, honey," Linda said softly.

"Mom, do you think I'm fat?" Sandy asked with tears rolling down her cheeks.

"I think you're beautiful. I think you are a wonderful daughter," Linda replied. She knew she had not really answered the question.

"That's not what I asked you, Mom," Sandy persisted. "You do think I'm fat, don't you?"

Linda knew her daughter needed her help. She took a deep breath. "Sandy, the thing that bothers me is that you seem unhappy with yourself. I love you for who you are. I don't judge you based on how much you weigh."

"Do you think I should lose weight?" Sandy would not let it go.

"Are you happy with yourself, sweetheart?" Linda was not going to deal with this problem as if it had to do with a number of pounds. "Do you feel that you are taking care of yourself the way you want? Are you happy with how you are dealing with your appearance?"

"No. I hate how I look. I can't stand how I look in clothes," Sandy said. "I hate myself for being such a pig."

"I don't like when you insult yourself," Linda replied. "If you are unhappy with yourself, then you need to make some changes. I am not concerned about your weight. I want you to feel good about yourself. If you are unhappy, I want you to figure out what you need to change. What do you think you should do?"

"I hate being fat, but I still eat potato chips and cookies," Sandy said. "I sit around like a slug. I tell myself that I should try to lose weight, but then I don't do it."

Linda told Sandy that she felt guilty for her role in this dilemma. "It was my job when you were younger to help you learn better habits. I think I let you down by not insisting that you eat healthier and exercise. I'm sorry that I didn't do a better job of that. But don't misunderstand me, I really do think you are beautiful and wonderful."

"Thanks, Mom."

"I think the problem now is that you feel like you have let yourself down," Linda continued. "You want to have healthier habits. You know it's good for you to eat better and exercise. You think you should do these things, but you don't do them. I don't think that you will feel good about yourself until you follow through on what you believe is right."

"I do feel awful," Sandy replied. "I feel like a hypocrite. I tell myself to be more conscious of how I eat and that I should exercise, but then I keep pigging out."

"I'm proud of you for realizing this about yourself," Linda said with a bit of a smile. "It's not easy for anyone to be honest about their faults. The problem is not your weight. You are letting yourself down by not following through on how you want to live your life."

Sandy was listening intently. She seemed to feel a little better. "You know, Mom, you're right. I don't like feeling this way about myself. I wish I could live the last five years over again and take care of myself better."

"Sweetheart, you're only 15," Linda laughed. "You have plenty of time to change."

"I think we should buy the blue dress. Do you think that one looked okay on me?" Sandy asked.

"I think you'll look beautiful."

Therapeutic Parenting will help you to take responsibility for teaching your child to handle challenges and problems. Hold yourself accountable for your actions as a parent. Be honest in your self-appraisal. Take action to change your parenting if you are dissatisfied. You will feel better about yourself and will model the best way for your child to have good self-esteem.

Key Points to Remember

- ❖ Validate your child.
- ❖ Hold him accountable.
- ❖ Teach her honest self-appraisal.
- ❖ Hold yourself to these same standards.

Chapter 13

Peer Pressure

Margaret pulled into a parking space at the shopping mall to wait for her 12-year-old daughter Emily, who was shopping with friends. Her daughter was supposed to be ready by 3 P.M., but it was now 3:15, and she was still nowhere in sight. Margaret was annoyed, but also a bit concerned. This was only Emily's second time going to the mall with friends without adult supervision. Margaret was relieved when she finally saw her daughter coming toward the car.

"Mom, you have to come into the mall," Emily said as she opened the passenger side door. She looked upset.

"What are you talking about, Emily? We have to go," Margaret responded.

"Mom, would you please just come with me!" Emily closed the car door and started to walk toward the mall.

Margaret hurried after her daughter. "Just a minute, Em," she said as she took her daughter's arm to slow her down. "What's the matter?"

"One of the store managers wants to talk to you. He said I was trying to steal a CD, and if you didn't come in with me, he was going to call the police."

Margaret could see that Emily had tears in her eyes, even though she was looking at the ground. "I don't believe this," Margaret said. "You didn't take a CD, did you?"

"I don't know, Mom."

"What do you mean, you don't know?" Margaret demanded. "Did you take a CD or not?"

"Well, I wasn't really going to steal it, Mom. The other kids took one, and they dared me to take one, too. I didn't take one at first, but then they called me a chicken. They said if I ever wanted to go to the mall with them again, I would have to go back and take one."

"So you did steal it! I can't believe you would ever steal something."

"Mom, I'm sorry." Emily was looking at her mother now, hoping to see some sign that she might accept her apology. But Margaret was not ready to let her daughter off the hook.

"I raised you to be honest. I'm shocked that you would break the law. I trusted you to go to the mall with your friends and be responsible."

Emily shrugged her shoulders and stared at the pavement.

"Why did you do this?" her mother persisted.

"I didn't want my friends to think I was a chicken. All the kids take stuff from stores, Mom."

"That's what I thought," Margaret replied. "You just caved in to the peer pressure. A couple of kids call you a chicken, make a dare, and everything I taught you goes out the window?"

"I know it's wrong. I made a mistake. I said I was sorry."

"Well, that's not good enough," Margaret continued. "What else are you going to do so your friends will think you're cool? Will you smoke marijuana if they dare you?"

"Of course not, I ..."

"Will you skip school if they tell you they won't be your friends if you don't skip with them?"

"No, I ..."

"How can I ever trust you now that I know you give in to peer pressure so easily?" Margaret was stunned that all of her emphasis on values and teaching her daughter to do the right things were so quickly undone by a couple of Emily's friends.

They walked into the mall and headed for the music store. Margaret was humiliated and furious. "Don't even think about asking me to go to the mall again, and you can forget going to the dance this weekend. I can't trust you with these friends of yours."

"Mom, please! I have to go to the dance."

"Forget it. You're grounded."

"For how long, Mom?"

"Until I can trust you, and I don't know when that will be."

Parents worry about peer pressure for good reason. Acceptance by peers is a powerful need. Some children will abandon what they have learned from their parents in order to be liked by friends. These children will ignore their values and make poor choices in a desperate attempt to gain acceptance. Peer pressure is the most likely cause of children engaging in high-risk behaviors such as drug use or driving under the influence.

All children want to be popular and have friends. When children choose good role models, peer pressure can be helpful. If a child's friends are well behaved, motivated in school, and respectful of others, then peer pressure is actually beneficial. These children want to fit in by being successful and responsible. All parents hope their children will find these kinds of friends.

Sadly, most parents feel that it is getting more difficult to find positive role models. More and more children seem to be growing up too fast, taking risks, using drugs and alcohol, having sex, and underachieving in school. The best predictor of whether a child will use drugs or drink alcohol is whether his friends do these things. Unfortunately, some of the most popular kids in today's society are the ones who engage in the very behaviors that parents fear most. These high-status peers are often seen as adventurous, bold, attractive, and exciting. Some children, who hope to be one of the "cool" kids, will engage in behaviors that violate parental values to achieve this status and acceptance.

The Pressure to Conform

Teaching a child to cope with peer pressure is not easy. Even strong-willed children with good values want to be accepted by peers. Fitting in with a group is so crucial to children's happiness and self-esteem that even these "good kids" from good families can be led astray. Parents are usually flabbergasted to see how easily all of their conscientious parenting can be undone in a matter of minutes. It's disheartening to parents to realize how susceptible their children are to the influence of peers.

Peer pressure begins at an early age. Even young children respond to feedback from peers and try to emulate the behavior of friends. A colleague of mine, who is a vegetarian, told me how her five-year-old son was feeling the effects of peer pressure. She sent him to camp each day with a vegetarian meal in his lunchbox. Her son was being teased that his lunches were "yucky." Her son complained so intensely that she finally relented and began sending more typical lunch fare.

Some parents raise their children from an early age to think independently and resist conformity. While these children are less susceptible to being led astray, they are not necessarily happy in the role of nonconformist. Having close friends and conforming to peer expectations are essential developmental needs. The desire to belong does not subside even when conscientious parents educate their children about the risks of peer pressure. For this reason, most parents struggle to find a balance between teaching their children how to avoid peer pressure while still learning to fit in with a group.

Therapeutic Parenting can help you teach your child to be less vulnerable to peer pressure. While there is no way to raise a child who is immune to its influence, you can help her be prepared for the inevitable situations where she is at risk. Inoculating your child against the adverse effects of negative role models begins with developing a strong parent-child relationship and teaching her your values.

The Positive Side of Peer Pressure

Peer pressure generally has a negative connotation. Sometimes, however, it can be very helpful, such as in the following scenarios:

- ❖ Friends stop a friend from making a mistake like drinking and driving.
- ❖ Actors, athletes, and musicians provide positive role models by living according to strong values.
- ❖ Popular teens show compassion for less fortunate classmates.
- ❖ Children belong to constructive groups, teams, or religious organizations.
- ❖ People rally around a cause such as combating homelessness.
- ❖ Students show school spirit by rooting for their athletic teams.

There are four steps to help your child learn to deal with peer pressure. While it's beneficial to introduce these techniques when your child is young, these steps will become a key component of your parenting by the time your child has entered adolescence. It is during this phase that the power of peer pressure and its associated risks are the greatest.

Step #1: Clarify Your Own Values About Popularity

How important is it for your child to be popular with peers? Some parents believe that having high social status is a key ingredient to their child's happiness. These parents think that a certain amount of conformity is necessary for their children to fit in with the group. Other parents believe that conformity for the sake of being liked is a sign of moral weakness. These parents value independent thought and action and frown upon conformity for the sake of popularity. Each of these perspectives has merit. Most parents seek a balance between these two points of view.

The first step in helping your child deal with peer pressure is for you to be clear about what you believe. Remember that your values will be taught both by what you tell your child and by how you act. Some parents give inconsistent messages about acceptance by peers by saying one thing but doing another. For example, some parents tell their children that they don't want them to be unduly influenced by what others think. However, these same parents may convey their desire that their children be popular. These parents may also be preoccupied with their own social success and with what others think of them.

Here are some of the reasons parents struggle to find the right balance between helping their children gain acceptance from friends versus being swayed by peer pressure.

When Parents Worry Too Much

One reason that some parents are confused about how to deal with peer pressure is fear. Few issues trigger greater anxiety, since all parents worry their children will be misled by someone else's child. Unfortunately, dangerous and traumatic events can occur when a child succumbs to peer pressure. Parents read newspaper stories chronicling foolish pranks that have gone too far, fraternity hazing that ends in tragedy, or young girls who have been sexually exploited by older boys. All parents dread getting a late-night phone call informing them that their child has been in a car accident or has been arrested by police.

Some parents deal with these fears by severely restricting how much peer contact they allow. Parents who are excessively worried attempt to regulate where their children go, what they do, and who they can have as friends. These parents hope to fend off danger by preventing their children from being in a situation where bad things can happen. While these parents may succeed in preventing their children from making some bad choices, these children are often unhappy with their parents and isolated from peers. When other kids are socializing or exploring independent activities, these kids are with their parents under surveillance. It's difficult for parents to maintain a warm relationship with children who resent them for getting in the way of their friendships and their growth toward independence.

Here are some of the characteristics of parents who are overly worried about their children getting into trouble. These parents ...

- ❖ Have overly restrictive rules compared to other parents. These kids have less ability to see friends, talk on the phone, use the Internet, or go out without supervision.

- ❖ Express their fears of what can go wrong if children have too much freedom: "You might be abducted if you go the mall. There are a lot of perverts out there who might kidnap you."

❖ Tell their children that they don't trust them to resist peer pressure: "You think you won't be led astray. But all kids, including you, will give in to peer pressure."

Examine your worries about your child. Make sure you do not let your fears cause you to be so restrictive that your child cannot develop appropriate peer relationships. For your child to learn to make good choices, she needs to practice using her own values to guide her. If she is always under your supervision, this will delay her developing the ability to rely on her own judgment.

When Parents Resent Conformity

Some parents have disdain for conformity. They see following a crowd as a distasteful personal weakness. They believe it is their responsibility to teach their children to actively challenge conformity. These parents are proud to be different from the norm. They hope their children will share this philosophy. When their children mindlessly follow the crowd, these parents are displeased.

Some parents develop this resentment toward conformity based on mistakes they made when they were teens. They feel guilt and regret for their own errors in judgment that adversely affected their lives. Perhaps as teenagers they began having sex too early or got pregnant, were arrested for something they did wrong while drinking, or failed in school, leading them to feel they wasted their education. These parents may be determined not to let their children make the same mistakes.

Parents who have these regrets often blame peer pressure for triggering their problems. They become overly diligent in criticizing conformity. They say, "I remember what I did when I was a kid, and I don't want my child to do the same things." These parents begin teaching their children at an early age to make their own decisions and not go along with the crowd.

210

This attitude has one major advantage: These children think independently and are less susceptible to peer pressure. However, this approach can be taken too far, and these children often have trouble fitting in when conformity is necessary. While they may not be influenced by peer pressure, they do have difficulty conforming to authority. They may refuse to accept regulations from teachers, especially if they think the rules are unfair or arbitrary.

Parents who prioritize independent thought are often surprised by how difficult it is to control their children as teenagers. These parents have done such a thorough job of indoctrinating their children to think for themselves that they don't listen to their parents, either! These children do what they think is right. Not only will they buck the influence of peers, they will also question the rules of teachers and the authority of parents.

Here are some of the characteristics of parents who go too far in preventing conformity. These parents …

* Criticize all conformity. They believe that conformity reflects dependence and vulnerability to peer pressure. These parents may say, "I can't believe you want to buy that skirt just because other kids are wearing it. Don't you have a mind of your own?"

* Put down the desire to be liked. These parents make their children feel badly if they try to be popular. "You seem to care too much about being liked. You need to like and respect yourself and stop caring so much about what other kids think."

* Make negative comments about popular children and their families. These parents seem to disrespect people who are socially minded. "I hope you don't want to be like John. He is so shallow, just like his father. All they care about is looking good."

211

Memories of Adolescent Rejection

Some parents remain highly sensitive about painful experiences they had when they were children. They vividly remember the social isolation and ostracism they felt from peers. Being rejected as a child, especially as a teenager, can be so hurtful that some adults are still sensitive years later. For these parents, the emotional scars of childhood rejection have not healed. Women may recall being teased about being fat or unattractive. Men may recall a derogatory nickname or being picked on for not being athletic.

As a testament to the damage done by these childhood experiences, some parents are determined to protect their children from this kind of pain. As parents, they try to prevent their children from being hurt. They will do anything to help their children be accepted and popular. Problems arise when parents are obsessed with their children's social success. When children are raised believing that it's essential to be popular, they are more vulnerable to peer pressure.

If you had some tough experiences with peers when you were a child, make sure you don't let those experiences override your values. You need to do what's best for your child, and not be confused by your own sensitivities. Here are some of the ways parents communicate their fear that their children will not be popular. These parents ...

❖ Make sure their children wear the right clothes and dress like other kids. These parents are very conscious that their children follow the latest trends. They monitor fads to ensure their kids are ready to join the crowd: "You don't want to wear those shoes, do you? All the kids are wearing these sneakers."

❖ Give their children feedback about the importance of being liked. These parents preface feedback to their children with the phrase, "If you want other kids to like you ..."

❖ Push their children to hang out with popular peers. These parents imply that popular kids make the best friends: "Why don't you invite John over the house tomorrow? He seems like such a great kid."

❖ Get overinvolved with discussions about friends and give advice about how to get ahead socially: "You should tell Tracy to mind her own business. She is just jealous of you because you are so popular. Don't hang out with her anymore. She is holding you back."

❖ Push their kids to get involved in sports and other extracurricular activities, even if their children don't want to participate: "You really should try out for the school play. It's a great way for you to develop a good reputation at school."

You need to clarify your values about how much conformity is good for your child and how far she should go to be popular. Be careful about being at the extreme of either perspective. Children who are too concerned with fitting in are more vulnerable to make poor choices based on peer pressure. Children who are raised to be nonconformists or fiercely independent may become socially isolated, unhappy, and resistant to authority. Figure out where you stand on this continuum and communicate your values to your child by what you say and, more importantly, by how you act.

Step #2: Prepare Your Child for Conflicts Between Family Values and Peer Pressure

It is inevitable your child will face situations where his wish to please others and the values you taught him will be in conflict. The key point of this step is for your child to be ready to identify these situations when they happen. Your child needs to recognize the dilemma as it is occurring and before he makes a mistake. This is a challenging task for your child, since most of these moments happen spontaneously and never occur when a parent is present. However, when that moment arrives, he has to make an important decision. He has to choose between what you have taught him and what his friends are urging him to do. Your job is to help him be ready to identify this decision point when it counts.

Since you know what kinds of conflicts are likely to occur, you need to talk to your child before she is in the middle of a situation. Many parents don't have these conversations because they can be awkward. Most kids don't like these talks either. It's hard for parents not to lecture and preach about these potential problems:

- ❖ Drug use
- ❖ Alcohol use
- ❖ Driving responsibly
- ❖ Sex
- ❖ Misdemeanors such as shoplifting and minor vandalism
- ❖ Being present when other kids are committing unlawful acts
- ❖ Telling the truth about where they are going

All teenagers will encounter some of these situations. Don't wait until after they occur to discuss them with your child. Prepare your child for how she must respond when other kids are doing these things. Develop plans for what she will do. Tell her you want her to recognize when she is in this situation and carry out the plans you have discussed.

Make sure you are comfortable with the plans you develop. A family once brought their 16-year-old son to me because he was having sex with his girlfriend. The son explained that his parents had told him several months earlier about the risks of sexually transmitted diseases and getting a girl pregnant. His parents gave him a box of a dozen condoms and told him to use them whenever he had sex. The boy was surprised that his parents were upset with him. He said, "I did exactly what you told me. I used a condom every time we had sex."

His parents were embarrassed when their son told me this story. They acknowledged that their son had done exactly what they recommended. Then his father added weakly, "We just didn't expect him to use up the condoms so quickly."

These parents thought they had conveyed their values by giving their son the condoms. Certainly they gave him an important message about safe sex. However, they omitted from their message that they also wanted him to wait until he was emotionally mature for sexual intimacy. They also did not talk to their son about the implications for his girlfriend of having sex. They were taken by surprise by their son's behavior. However, they took a shortcut that left out a discussion of values.

What Teenagers Say About Peer Pressure

Most teenagers are aware that they are susceptible to peer pressure. Here are some of the reasons they give for why they seek acceptance or take risks. These teens ...

* Want to be liked.
* Are not comfortable being seen as different from peers.
* Are worried they will be teased or embarrassed.
* Are confused about their own beliefs.
* Are trying to have fun.
* Want to create an image or identity.
* Are making a statement about rejecting the values of society.
* Do not believe bad things will happen to them if they take risks.
* Realize they are in a phase and that they will grow out of it.

TLC is a useful model for you to discuss issues of peer pressure. You can share values, discuss options, and develop plans. If your child is reluctant to participate in these conversations, try a monologue. Here is an example:

"I'm glad you're getting along with your friends. They seem to like you and I can tell you like them. You're getting to an age when having friends and being popular can be a really strong need. Some of your decisions might be made based on how other kids will feel about you, which is how peer pressure works. That's normal and nothing to feel bad about.

"Sometimes, though, your friends may do things that aren't consistent with our family values. When your friends put pressure on you to go against your values, I want you to be very careful. At that moment, you really need to think clearly about what is the best thing to do. For example, let's say that one of your friends wants you to smoke some pot. At that moment, no matter how strongly you are tempted to do what your friends are pushing you to do, you have to realize that smoking pot is illegal. Remember that we can talk about this if you want, and I can help you figure out what to do."

The solutions you develop with your child must ensure that her social needs are being met while still having her adhere to your values. Remember that no issue is worth losing the warmth in your relationship. Your ability to limit the negative impact of peer pressure depends on remaining close to your child.

Step #3: Problem Solve Around Minor Errors in Judgment

This step concerns how to deal with mistakes children may make due to peer pressure in which they have not actually put themselves in danger. Serious mistakes in judgment where your child is at high risk will be covered in Step 4.

When children succumb to peer pressure, parents are often disappointed and even angry. Parents may respond to these mistakes with limits or lectures. They worry that if their child is vulnerable to peer pressure about a small thing, like insisting on wearing the same kind of jeans a friend wears, that the child will also give in to temptation on bigger issues. This is not necessarily true. Most children understand that there is a big difference between copying a fad and violating a major family value such as stealing from a neighbor.

If your child makes a mistake and inappropriately gives in to peer pressure, this is an opportunity to teach your child a lesson about values. If he thinks you will lecture him, restrict his freedom, or make him feel bad about his choices, he will stop communicating. Remember that your child needs you to be sensitive, caring, and helpful. These small mistakes are a chance to work on problem solving and to strengthen values used to resist peer pressure.

Most kids know when they have made a mistake. Before you tell your child what she did wrong, give her a chance to tell you what she thinks about her actions. Ask her questions that will help her to examine her own behavior. Here are the kinds of questions that will help her to reflect on her choices:

"Do you feel what you did was right?"

"What was the most important thing to you at the time you made your decision?"

"How much were you concerned about what your friends were thinking?"

"Would you have done the same thing if your friends were not there or not encouraging you to do this?"

"How did you feel after you did this?"

"What could you have done instead?"

Here are several techniques that, with practice, will help your child make better choices in the future:

❖ Remind your child to stop and think before he acts. Many mistakes that result from peer pressure are impulsive. When children take a few moments to think about what they are doing, they are less likely to make a poor choice.

217

❖ Identify situations that are obvious places that peer pressure might be a problem. For example, if your child is going on an overnight class trip, discuss what she will do under certain circumstances (for example, if the other kids suggest they sneak into each other's rooms at night).

❖ Discuss what your child can say when he refuses to go along with peer pressure. Many children do not want to do the wrong thing, but panic when they don't know what to say to get out of the situation. Practice what your child can say that is comfortable for him. His response may be something as simple as, "You go ahead. I'll pass on this one."

❖ Talk about her responsibility to be a leader to her friends by showing others that it is okay not to go along with the crowd. Your child may not realize that she will be more respected and popular if he is seen as a strong person who makes his own decisions. He should also be ready to help a friend who is making a bad decision, such as getting in a car with a driver who has been drinking.

❖ Develop an exit strategy for how he can get out of a difficult situation. For example, if he is at a party that is getting too wild, he can always call you to pick him up.

Most of the time, discussion and problem solving using Therapeutic Parenting are sufficient to help a child learn to deal with peer pressure. Even if a child makes mistakes, this model allows you to help your child learn to handle these situations. The exception to this process is when your child is succumbing to peer pressure and is involved with situations where she is at high risk. In these circumstances, you will need to use the next step to deal with these serious problems.

Step #4: Identify Areas That Put Your Child at High Risk and Set Limits

Some forms of conformity are more dangerous than others. You will need to help your child sort out which kinds of peer pressure put him at high risk. The behaviors that you perceive as a risk for your child will depend on his age. Since most of the serious problems with peer pressure occur with teens, let's look at what types of behavior are lower risk or higher risk for this age group. While not all parents would categorize these actions in the same way, here is one example of what many parents would include as lower risk:

❖ Wanting to dress like friends

❖ Talking the same way

❖ Listening to similar music

❖ Wanting to spend time with friends doing similar activities

❖ Being in a clique

While these activities can lead to more serious forms of at-risk behavior, most children can deal with this level of peer pressure without getting into trouble. Some children go beyond these activities and are exposed to high-risk peer pressure, including friends who ...

❖ Drink alcohol.

❖ Use drugs.

❖ Have sex.

❖ Commit illegal acts.

❖ Fail or seriously underachieve in school.

❖ Engage in self-damaging acts such as cutting themselves.

These are the high-risk behaviors that all parents fear. Some parents make the mistake, however, of responding similarly to low-risk and high-risk activities. Part of your job is to differentiate these behaviors. Don't try to stop all signs of conformity or socialization with peers. This overly restrictive approach will make your child see you as unfair, insensitive to his needs, and out of touch with what is normal for most teens.

On the other hand, your child needs to get a crystal-clear picture of what behaviors are unacceptable and dangerous. You will need to take strong action to prevent those high-risk behaviors that are a real threat to your child's well-being. This is another example of learning to pick your battles. For high-risk behaviors, you need to be firm and direct about how you view these behaviors and what you will do in response.

Your reaction to high-risk behavior needs to be different than anything else you have learned in Therapeutic Parenting. You still need to listen empathetically, protect your relationship, and find solutions. However, when it comes to these dangerous behaviors, you will need to be directive, to set limits, and to act unilaterally to protect your child's well-being. If you have been consistently flexible, supportive, and warm about other issues, when you need to be firm and restrictive about these high-risk behaviors, your child will be more likely to comply.

Use your judgment in deciding how risky a particular situation is to your child. Don't switch into the limit-setting mode unless you have identified the potential for danger. This assessment can be difficult. For example, let's say your 15-year-old daughter wants to go to a party. Should you let her go? If there will be adult supervision at the party and you know that the other kids are a responsible group of friends, then you will probably feel comfortable saying yes. On the other hand, if you know there will be no adult supervision and that some of the kids going to the party are likely to drink and use drugs, then this is too much risk to allow your 15-year-old child to go.

Where parents draw the line about how much risk is acceptable varies depending upon the child's age, community, and many other factors. You will have to decide when your child has crossed the line and when you need to dictate what your child can and cannot do.

You will also have to decide what kinds of sanctions you will impose when your child engages in high-risk behaviors. For example, let's say that you found out your 16-year-old son was smoking marijuana and hanging out with kids who had serious drug problems. Here are some examples of the kinds of limits and actions to consider:

* Limiting his ability to be unsupervised with peers
* Calling other parents to make sure he is at the location he said he was going to and that there is an adult present
* Having an earlier curfew
* Taking away his privilege to drive
* Identifying peers he is not allowed to see outside of school
* Letting him know you will search his room to look for drugs
* Taking him to a psychologist for treatment
* Getting drug screens to determine if he is still using marijuana or other drugs

This list is very different from anything else that appears in this book. The message to your child is that high-risk behaviors will be treated differently than any other problem. This doesn't mean that you will abandon the key components of Therapeutic Parenting. You should still try to remain caring and connected to your child. You should explain your values. You should encourage him to express his point of view. However, he should also see clearly that dangerous behavior requires you to take a stand. You will not feel comfortable with yourself if you don't try to prevent your child from being harmed.

Here is a monologue for how to explain this course of action:

"I'm worried about you and disappointed in your actions. I think you have put yourself at risk and have used bad judgment. I love you and know that you can learn to be more careful, but for now, I don't think you're ready to be responsible. I'm going to set up a new set of rules. These aren't punishments. They are limits to help you stay safe and not get in trouble. I want to talk to you about this problem. I'll be ready to make changes in these rules when I'm comfortable knowing that I can be sure you will not put yourself in danger."

If you have always been fair and flexible with your child, he will see your actions as reasonable given the gravity of his poor judgment. He will understand that you have always tried to include him when seeking solutions to less serious problems. However, now you have to take action to prevent him from making a dangerous mistake. His safety is not negotiable.

Eve and her mother disagreed about what the real problem was. Her mother, Tracy, believed the problem was that their 16-year-old daughter was making herself throw up. Tracy was worried she had developed an eating disorder.

Eve believed the problem was that her mother was too restrictive. For example, Eve thought it was ludicrous that she had never been to a party. She had stopped even asking her mother if she could go to the parties at her friends' homes.

Tracy was very traditional and protective. Eve's father had died when Eve was a baby. Tracy felt enormous responsibility to make sure she protected her daughter. She was alarmed by what she saw happening in today's culture. She believed the risks were enormous for Eve. She worried about drugs and alcohol. She worried about sex and felt that Eve was too young to date. She did not allow her to be in a car driven by other teenagers. She did not let her walk in the neighborhood unsupervised out of concern that she might be abducted by a stranger.

Eve had become increasingly unhappy. When she was younger, some of her friends had similar rules. Now her life was more restricted than any of her friends. Eve showed her anger by being sullen and disagreeable. She refused to do chores. Her room was a mess. When she was younger, Eve would tell her mother about her friends and what she did at school, but her communication had stopped. Eve was too angry to discuss anything with her mother.

When Tracy first suspected Eve was throwing up, her daughter denied it. However, as the days passed, Tracy saw telltale signs in the bathroom. She confronted Eve again, and her daughter finally admitted she was making herself vomit.

Tracy and Eve came to see me, but Tracy had a very different agenda than Eve. Tracy wanted to help her daughter stop vomiting. Eve, on the other hand, wanted to have a happier life. She felt she was in prison under her mother's restrictive rules. She stated emphatically that she threw up when she could not cope with the anger she felt toward her mother for not giving her more freedom.

Tracy was initially adamant about not changing her rules. She felt that Eve, like all other children, was at risk by associating with friends who did not share their values. While she understood that Eve was unhappy, she felt her displeasure was a necessary side effect of her decision to protect her from danger.

Eve was particularly frustrated that her mother did not believe in her. She had never done anything seriously wrong. She had never smoked a cigarette, used marijuana or alcohol, or gone to a party without permission. She was planning to go to college in two years and was worried that she would suddenly be thrust into a totally different world for which she felt unprepared.

Tracy admitted that she was scared to change the way she treated Eve. She lived in fear that something dreadful would happen to her daughter. She had a hard time coping with her own morbid fantasies of Eve being killed in a car accident or abducted by a stranger. These fears were at the bottom of her reluctance to give Eve more freedom. She saw Eve's peers as the greatest threat to her daughter's safety. Giving her daughter the freedom to be with peers terrified Tracy. She worried her sheltered daughter would rapidly fall under their influence. She foresaw every imaginable problem resulting from peer pressure: drinking, driving dangerously, and having sex.

As Tracy looked more honestly at the reasons for her restrictive rules, she realized that her decisions were not really in her daughter's best interest. These rules were to protect herself. The strict guidelines allowed Tracy to cope with her own anxieties. She had convinced herself that this was really the best thing for Eve. Now, she was beginning to truly think about what her daughter needed.

Tracy agreed to learn Therapeutic Parenting and to talk to Eve about her feelings. Tracy's worries about Eve developing a serious eating disorder motivated her to reassess her parenting style.

The two of them began a process of discussing their values and feelings and looking at possible solutions to their problem. Eve was not asking for a lot of changes. She wanted permission to begin dating boys, to talk on the phone until 10 P.M., and to attend some parties. She agreed to not drink, use drugs, or stay in any situation that she thought was risky. Tracy agreed she would pick Eve up any time she called if she felt she was in an unacceptable situation. Eve agreed she would try to stop making herself vomit.

This transition was difficult for Tracy. She struggled to deal with her own anxieties. She began individual therapy to discuss her fears and how she could cope with them. Eve, however, was much happier. She stopped vomiting. She slowly began to talk to her mother about her life and her feelings.

Helping your child deal with peer pressure is one of your greatest challenges. You will have to exercise careful judgment about how much freedom to allow your child, given that he lives in a fast-paced world with many poor role models. Despite these risks, you can help him find solutions that allow him to be part of a peer group while remaining true to the values you have taught him.

Key Points to Remember

❖ Seeking acceptance is a normal part of development.

❖ Parents' own experiences affect their reaction to peer pressure.

❖ Errors in judgment are great opportunities for learning.

❖ Set limits on high-risk behaviors.

Chapter 14

In Conclusion: A Few More Thoughts About Teenagers

"Dad, I need the car tonight," Hank said. "I'm going over to Billy's house, and then we're going to the movies."

"Well, you can't have the car tonight," Stuart, his father, replied. "You said you would mow the lawn today, and you didn't. I'm tired of you not following through on your responsibilities."

"Come on, Dad. I'll mow the lawn tomorrow."

"No. You heard me. It's always tomorrow with you, but tomorrow never comes."

Stuart was frustrated with Hank. His son was so wrapped up with his friends that he ignored his chores and his schoolwork. Hank had also become disrespectful whenever he didn't get what he wanted. Stuart braced himself for what he knew was coming next.

"Screw you," Hank muttered.

"I'm sick of that attitude, son." Stuart tried to sound calm, but he was angry. "You are not allowed to talk to me that way."

"Well, you suck," his son hissed. "You use the car as a weapon. You always threaten me with it. Just take your car and shove it." Hank stormed out of the house.

Stuart could not believe his son talked to him this way. Hank used to be polite and loving. Now, he was angry and disrespectful. Stuart actually felt a bit afraid of him. He was not worried that Hank would hurt him. He was worried his son would do something stupid if he became too angry. Stuart found himself giving in to avoid confrontations. He had largely stopped reminding Hank about chores and schoolwork, because he did not want to set off one of his son's outbursts.

Stuart wondered what could have caused Hank to change into this moody, trash-talking stranger who he barely recognized as his son. Could he be taking drugs? Was he in some kind of trouble? Was he being influenced by friends to rebel? Stuart had no answers as to what caused this transformation.

Stuart did not look forward to Hank's returning after his outburst. He wasn't sure what to do. Part of him wanted to confront his son and lay down the law. However, he was concerned this would lead to the kind of escalation that Stuart feared most. Another part of Stuart wanted to hug Hank and ask him what was wrong. However, he worried his son would rebuff him and merely use this as an occasion to get what he wanted—the car.

A banging sound jarred Stuart out of his ruminations. Hank had reentered the house and kicked the door to his bedroom closed. Stuart heard loud, angry music blare from the stereo in his son's bedroom. Stuart hoped that Hank would not come out for a long time.

Many parents worry about what will happen when their children reach adolescence. There is the common belief that adolescence is always a time of rebellion and conflict between parents and teenagers. While conflict does arise in some families, this pattern is far from universal. Many parents remain close to their children throughout the teen years. Some parents even find raising teenagers to be the most rewarding part of parenting. Therapeutic Parenting is designed to ensure that you never feel estranged from your child, including when he is a teenager.

Adolescence is the period when children are at the greatest risk to get into trouble and make bad choices. Teenagers are the most susceptible to influence by peers. They usually believe they are mature and ready to make their own choices. They certainly are more capable than younger children, and this includes having greater ability to defy parents.

Dangers do exist for adolescents. Teens can be led astray. Raising children today is more challenging than ever before because of the risks that exist in our culture. Most parents worry about getting their children safely through the teen years. Therapeutic Parenting will help prevent your child from being unduly influenced by inappropriate role models.

Your Changing Role As a Parent

If you raise your child using Therapeutic Parenting, your child will grow up knowing your values and will internalize them. Instead of rejecting your beliefs, she will integrate your values into the way she leads her life. She will be less susceptible to negative peer pressure. As a teenager, your child will begin the process of making more independent decisions. However, she will do this while still feeling close to you and knowing right from wrong.

On the other hand, if your relationship is seriously damaged, your teenager will feel alienated from you and your values. If he rebels in anger, he will adopt values and behaviors that are the opposite of what you have taught him. Preventing this alienation is crucial. Using Therapeutic Parenting is like inoculating your child against disease. It ensures that your child will be immune to many of the problems that teenagers encounter.

Your goal is to be flexible when your child becomes a teenager. You will need to give her more opportunities to make her own decisions and solve her own problems. She needs to practice what you have taught her by using her values to find her way. When she has difficulties, discuss her choices using TLC. Help her to analyze her actions and honestly examine her successes and failures.

Your role must evolve from being a parent who regulates and structures his life to a caring consultant who helps him learn and grow from his experiences. This transition on your part must be gradual and appropriate to his age and level of maturity. However, by the time your child is 16 or 17, this transition should be mostly complete. By this time, you should no longer rely heavily on limits, punishment, or routines to regulate your child. While you will occasionally need to resort to these strategies, older teenagers will feel stifled by these techniques. Over-regulating teenagers leads to alienation and rebellion. Since your relationship is always the highest priority, you will need to soften your approach to guarantee that you remain close.

Some parents have difficulty relinquishing control of their teenagers. They fear that loosening the reins will lead to problems, since teenagers' lives are filled with temptations. It's true that some intelligent, good kids make bad choices. This reality makes it difficult for some parents to let go of their control. These parents hope to keep their children safe until adolescence is over. The problem with this thinking is that children need to learn to regulate themselves. If they are not given an opportunity to practice taking care of themselves, they will not learn how to do it. When these sheltered teens are finally granted independence, they have difficulty functioning without supervision. They are not prepared to solve problems and make decisions on their own.

Therapeutic Parenting is value based for these reasons. Your child must internalize a set of values that he can use once he is on his own. These values are essential for him to make safe choices and to have a sense of direction. Combining his values with active problem solving will make your child self-sufficient. All children face challenges. Make sure you give your child the tools to make good choices and to learn from his mistakes.

Myths About Teens

Many people have misconceptions about today's teenagers. Here are some of the myths and realities:

Myth: All teenagers go through a rebellious phase.

Fact: Many teenagers never rebel or reject authority.

Myth: Teens pull away from their parents during adolescence.

Fact: Many teens feel they become closer to their parents during adolescence.

Myth: Teens are self-centered and can only think about themselves.

Fact: Many teens are highly sensitive to the needs of others and capable of remarkable compassion.

Myth: Teens are becoming less motivated academically.

Fact: Standardized test scores show teens are smarter than ever before, and competition for college acceptance is at an all-time high.

Adolescence is a chance for your child to gradually learn to take care of herself and still have you close by when she needs help. Her teen years offer an opportunity for her to practice what you have taught her. She will make plenty of mistakes. Don't worry about her bad choices or missed chances. Each of these experiences is an opportunity for you to discuss her decisions and to help her learn. She will learn the most from her mistakes. She will need you a great deal during this time—but not through regulation and control. She will need you in a different way. She will need your support and encouragement. She will need your wisdom.

Let's look at a typical scenario of how these issues play out with teenagers. Let's say your 16-year-old son has been offered a job after school and on weekends. He plans to work 18 hours a week. He is excited, because he wants to make money and save it to buy a car. You are concerned that this job is too much for him and will adversely affect his schoolwork. When he was younger, you would have appropriately told him he could not take the job; now, however, he is 16, and your role is different. As a consultant, it is your role to advise him and help him learn from his choices. You should ask him questions about how he will manage to meet his other responsibilities, including his school-work. You should also tell him what you think he should do. However, you should let him make his own decision. Here is a monologue that addresses these issues:

> "I know how much you want this job. I'm proud of you for want-
> ing to earn money and for being such a hard worker. I will let
> you make your own decision about this, but I do have an opinion.
> I'm worried this job is too much of a commitment. I think it'll
> interfere with your schoolwork. You only have one more year
> before you go to college. I think you're better off prioritizing
> your schoolwork. If you really want to work, I think you should
> look for a job that is less of a commitment. If you take this job, I
> think you should agree that if your grades suffer, you will quit the
> job. I trust you, but I'm worried that you're taking on too much."

These kinds of issues are very difficult for parents who are faced with a choice of giving their child independence versus taking control and preventing a mistake. Obviously, you must evaluate each situation for your child. Some mistakes are too serious, and you will need to step in to prevent them.

The idea is not to let your child make every decision and for you to end your role as parent. Instead, you need to gradually turn over the decision making to your child. You should, however, continue to discuss choices and values, and to express your opinion. You must remain an important part of this process as your child makes the transition to self-regulation.

Here are some guidelines for advising your teenager while still supporting his independence:

❖ Don't harshly criticize his mistakes. Help him to evaluate his choices honestly and learn from his errors. Do not make him fear your disapproval if he makes a bad decision. If he does, he will not want to discuss his mistakes with you.

❖ Discuss her options so she can fully examine her choices. Help her to look at the implications of each choice.

❖ Ask him questions about his choices. This will help him to be thorough in examining his decisions.

❖ Discuss your values and ask her what she believes is right. Remind her that values should be a key ingredient in every decision.

❖ Be empathic to his failures. Let him know that you feel bad about his lack of success. Do not tell him, "I told you so."

❖ Express confidence in her. Let her know you have faith that she will do the right thing. Tell her that even when she makes mistakes, you know she will work on solutions until the problem is solved.

❖ Express your feelings. This includes telling him why you are worried. Instead of explaining what is wrong with his plan, say, "I'm worried about what you're doing. I'm afraid that you'll end up unhappy with this decision."

❖ Recommend how to evaluate her choice. This may include a time frame for how long to wait before making a change or how she will know when she has made a bad choice: "If I'm too tired to do my homework after practice and my grades go down, I agree that I shouldn't stay on the team."

❖ Give him credit when his choices are good. Let him enjoy his success, even if you disagreed with what he did.

When parents don't follow these guidelines, their teenagers will be reluctant to be completely honest. Teens usually prefer to discuss their choices and problems with their parents, unless their parents make them regret their honesty. For example, let's say your teenage daughter says she is having conflict with a female friend. She says that her friend is seeing this guy who was arrested for possession of marijuana. Your daughter is worried that her girlfriend may get in trouble with this guy and wants to discuss it with you. However, when you hear the details, you're worried about your daughter's hanging around with this girl and her boyfriend. Your fear is that she will get in trouble by associating with her girlfriend. When she asks for your help about her friend, you say, "I don't want you hanging around with her anymore. She is going to get you in trouble. You are forbidden to see her again."

Your daughter will regret she ever told you the truth. She will feel that confiding in you was a mistake, since you are now setting limits on who she can have as friends. She will decide that the next time she has a difficult dilemma she had better look elsewhere for advice. Once this happens, you lose the ability to guide your child. You cannot be a moral adviser and help her learn from her mistakes, because she will not include you in the discussion.

Here is how you could respond to your daughter in this same scenario: "I'm glad you want to talk about this with me. I know how much you care about your friends. I'm proud of you for realizing that she may be making a bad decision and for wanting to help her. Now, you know that I'm worried about your friends making bad choices when you're with them. I trust you, but I worry about what other kids might do. So, let's try to figure out what you can do to help her."

Your goal is to maintain open communication throughout your child's teen years. Your child should never regret that he talked to you about any issue. This does not mean you always have to agree with your child. It means that your child must feel that you are a good listener and that you trust him.

Will Your Child Be Ready for College Life?

The biggest transition for most children leaving for college is getting used to the freedom. What are your rules and expectations about the following?

* **Curfews:** Most college students have no curfew.

* **Parties:** Most college students have no limitations on what parties they choose to attend.

* **Drinking:** Even though most are underage, the majority of college students drink alcohol.

* **Studying:** College students are on their own about finding time to study and completing assignments.

* **Friends:** College students quickly develop a new circle of friends, some of whom their parents will never meet.

* **Sex:** College students have the time, freedom, and opportunity to pursue sexual relationships.

Maintaining a Caring Connection

No issue is more important than being close to your child. During adolescence, parents have the greatest conflict in keeping this priority clear. Parents are easily confused by the intensity of competing priorities.

Here are the most common issues that can end up leading to conflict with teens:

* **Schoolwork.** College and careers are right around the corner. Teens are easily distracted from completing their schoolwork by peer relationships and the pursuit of pleasure.

* **Chores.** Parents battle with their adolescents over completing chores around the home. Rebellious teens often exert their autonomy by refusing to comply.

* **Curfew.** Most teens want to stay out later than parents find acceptable.

* **Dating.** Parents worry about whether their children are ready to handle relationships responsibly, especially regarding sex. Teens usually think they are ready.

* **Outside activities.** Teens want freedom to go to parties, drive in cars with friends, and go away for the weekend.

* **Respect.** Teens are often disrespectful in how they talk to their parents.

All of these issues are important. None is more critical than your relationship. If you have intense conflict over how to resolve your differences, you will damage your relationship and your child will feel alienated. You must find solutions to your disagreements while maintaining the connection with your child. If you get your way, but at the expense of a caring relationship, you won't be satisfied with the results. If your child complies, but is resentful and alienated, you'll lose your ability to influence your child in other situations. You may temporarily stop your teenager from engaging in unacceptable behavior, but she will eventually defy you and reject your lifestyle.

When you have disagreements over issues, seek a compromise that is acceptable to both you and your teen. Use the skills you have learned in Therapeutic Parenting to find solutions while remaining caring and close.

It's never too late to repair a relationship. If you and your teenage child are already alienated from one another, don't despair. You can reconnect with your child by using Therapeutic Parenting. Despite his overtly defiant attitude, he wants to be close to you. He may deny this out of immaturity or pride. However, don't be misled. Your teenager still needs your love and guidance.

The most common mistake that parents of alienated teens make is to insist that their children conform to expectations as the first step in repairing a relationship. These parents feel their children are so irresponsible or hurtful that the parents refuse to reach out to them. They will not be caring or warm until their teens show they are ready to act more respectfully. Certainly, some teens are highly oppositional and unpleasant. Their parents have had to endure months of angry and irresponsible behavior. It's understandable why these parents are unwilling to take action to improve their relationship. However, waiting for their children to become respectful as a condition for repairing the relationship is a mistake. These children are confused and are being influenced by powerful forces that they don't fully understand. Their view of reality is distorted by their egocentric, youthful perspectives. They think they are grown up and more wise than they actually are. However, these teens are still children. They are too immature to break the stalemate and reach out to their parents. These stalemates can last for years as parents wait for their child to be more responsible, and the adolescent remains defiant.

Don't let this happen to your family. You are the adult and have the maturity to end this stalemate. Never give up trying to reach out to your child. Always endeavor to repair a damaged relationship. Don't let pride or stubbornness prevent you from finding a solution that will lead to a close relationship with your child.

"Where were you tonight, Heather?" Ron asked. He knew the answer to the question, but was curious if his 17-year-old daughter would tell him the truth.

"I was over Ashley's house, Dad," Heather replied. "We watched a video and had some pizza."

"That's not true, honey. I got a call from Janet's father who said that there was a party at Gordon's house and that there was drinking. Janet's father said you were there."

Heather blushed. She had a frightened, pained look. Ron knew the truth just from looking at her face. He was shocked that Heather would lie to him. He had always trusted her. He thought she respected him enough that she would tell him the truth.

"Why did you lie to me, Heather?"

"I did go to Ashley's, Dad," Heather said. She was flustered. "We went to Gordon's afterward."

"Don't make this any worse than it already is, Heather. I don't want any more lies to cover up your tracks. You went to a party without permission, and you had no intention of telling me."

Heather was starting to get teary. "Dad, I am so sorry. I was at the party. I didn't mean to lie."

"What about the drinking?" Ron asked.

"Some kids were drinking. It wasn't some wild orgy or anything."

"Did you drink, Heather?"

"Dad, I took a few sips of someone else's beer," Heather explained. "Maybe I had a total of like a half of a beer."

Ron knew this was an important moment for him and his daughter. Heather was about to begin her senior year in high school. She was going to college next year. Ron was not naive. He knew kids went to parties where there was drinking. He remembered his own teenage years. He had done his share of partying. He had tried to impress upon his daughter how dangerous it was to drink,

236

especially if she was driving a car. Ron had also always stressed being honest. He was the most surprised and disappointed about Heather's lying to him.

"I have always trusted you and believed that you told me the truth, Heather," Ron said softly. "I am very disappointed in you for not being honest. Frankly, I'm shocked that you were trying to deceive me."

"Dad, I'm sorry," Heather was stung by her father's disapproval. "What was I supposed to do? Should I have said to you, 'Dad, I'm going to a party tonight and I'm going to drink some beer?'"

"Actually, yes," Ron said. "We should have talked about this. I think you owe it to me to be honest. If you're at a party, I want to know about it."

"If I had told you I was going to a party and there was going to be drinking, you would have told me that I couldn't go," Heather said.

"Well, maybe I would have said that," Ron responded. "But you didn't give me the chance to talk it over with you. Was it so important to go to this party that you felt you needed to lie about it?"

"Jeez, Dad. I said I was sorry. I feel bad enough already," Heather said. "But, yes. This party was very important to me. I really wanted to go. I knew I could handle myself. I didn't get drunk. I was responsible. I was worried that if I told you the truth I wouldn't get to go."

"Well, I am hurt and disappointed," Ron said. "The most important thing to me is that we have an honest relationship. What are we going to do about this?"

"You're right, Dad. I messed up. I shouldn't have lied."

"Okay, honey. So what happens the next time there's a party?"

"Dad, I think I'm ready to go to parties. I promise that I'll act responsibly. I won't get drunk. I'll never get in a car with a driver who has had anything to drink. Look, I would rather tell you the truth, but I don't want to be prevented from going if I'm honest about it."

Ron did trust Heather, despite her transgression. He certainly did worry about what could go wrong if he let her go to these parties. Even if she were responsible, it didn't mean the other kids would act that way. But if he gave her permission, wouldn't it condone her doing something illegal? How could he tell her it was okay? On the other hand, if he said she couldn't go, she would feel punished for her honesty. The reality was that soon she would be at college, and he knew there would be lots of parties. Wasn't Heather better off learning to be responsible now, while she still lived at home, so Ron could be there to help guide her?

"The most important thing to me," Ron said, "is that we talk this out and find a solution together. I am worried about your going to parties where there is drinking. I don't trust the other kids; you never know how they'll act when they drink too much."

"Dad, my friends are good kids."

"I know they are. But good kids get into trouble when they drink. I would rather you wait until you're older to be at parties where there's drinking. But I also have too much respect and faith in you to force you to do what I want."

"So you're saying that I can't go?" Heather asked, a note of disappointment in her voice.

"I'm saying I want you to be honest. I'm telling you what I believe is best. But I also believe in you. I will not punish you for going to a party. You aren't going to get grounded. If you go, I want to know where you are and when you'll be home."

"I promise that I won't lie to you again."

"I believe you. I expect us to keep talking about this, honey. I want to have a chance to tell you how I feel and what I think. Are you willing to do that?"

"Well, what if you don't like what you hear? What then?" Heather asked.

"I expect you to look honestly at your actions and for you and I to discuss them. If you make a mistake, I just want you to learn from it. Your safety is not something I take lightly."

Heather smiled. "Hey, look how much I've already learned from the mistake I just made."

Therapeutic Parenting is designed to help you deal with the confusing issues that all parents confront in raising children in today's complex world. Even though the world has changed and our children face many risks, it is still possible to raise emotionally healthy children. Being a parent is hard work. Therapeutic Parenting is a lot of work, too. However, your child is worth the effort.

Never give up until you find the right solutions to help your child. Model a style of problem solving that you want your child to learn. Be respectful and caring. Remain committed to your values and live your life by what you believe. Hold your child accountable to these values and help him to use these beliefs to regulate her actions. Never sacrifice a caring relationship. Be loving and caring no matter what obstacles develop. Follow these guidelines, and you will give your child what he needs to be an emotionally healthy and successful adult.

Key Points to Remember

❖ Teenagers still need your advice and encouragement.

❖ Gradually relinquish your control over your teenager.

❖ Never sacrifice a caring relationship over any issue.

❖ It's never too late to repair a damaged relationship.

Resources

Helpful Books for Parents (General)

Brazelton, T. Berry. *To Listen to a Child: Understanding the Normal Problems of Growing Up*. Reading, MA: Addison-Wesley, 1992.

————. *Touchpoints: Your Child's Emotional and Behavioral Development*. Reading, MA: Addison-Wesley, 1992.

Brazelton, T. Berry, and Stanley I. Greenspan. *Irreducible Needs of Children: What Every Child Must Have to Grow, Learn, and Flourish*. Cambridge: MA: Perseus Publications, 2000.

Butler, Shelley, and Deb Kratz. *Field Guide to Parenting: A Comprehensive Handbook of Great Ideas, Advice, Tips, and Solutions for Parenting Children Ages One to Five*. Worcester, MA: Chandler House Press, 1999.

Covey, Stephen R., and Sandra Merrill Covey. *The 7 Habits of Highly Effective Families: Building a Beautiful Family Culture in a Troubled World*. New York: Golden Books Publishers, 1997.

Davis, Laura, and Janis Keyser. *Becoming the Parent You Want to Be*. New York: Broadway Books, 1997.

Dinkmeyer, Dan, and Gary D. McKay. *Raising a Responsible Child: How to Prepare Your Child for Today's Complex World* (revised and updated edition). New York: Simon & Schuster, 1996.

Eisenberg, Nancy. *The Caring Child*. Cambridge, MA: Harvard University Press, 1992.

Elkind, David. *Miseducation: Preschoolers at Risk*. New York: Random House, Inc., 1987.

———. *Ties That Stress: The New Family Imbalance*. Cambridge, MA: Harvard University Press, 1994.

Ellis, Elizabeth. *Raising a Responsible Child: How Parents Can Avoid Overindulgent Behavior and Nurture Healthy Children*. Secaucus, NJ: Carol Publishing Group, 1995.

Joslin, Karen Renshaw. *Positive Parenting from A to Z*. New York: Ballantine Books, 1994.

Ludtke, Melissa. *On Our Own: Unmarried Motherhood in America*. New York: Random House, 1997.

Nelsen, Jane, and Stephen H. Glenn. *Positive Discipline*. New York: Ballantine Books, 1996.

Nelsen, Jane, Lynn Lott, and Stephen H. Glenn. *Positive Discipline A to Z, Revised and Expanded: From Toddlers to Teens, 1,001 Solutions to Everyday Parenting Problems*. Rocklin, CA: Prima Press, 1999.

Pruitt, David, ed. *Your Child: What Every Parent Needs to Know About Childhood Development from Birth to Preadolescence*. New York: HarperCollins, 1988.

Roker, Al. *Don't Make Me Stop This Car! Adventures in Fatherhood*. New York: Scribner, 2001.

Shure, Myrna B. *Raising a Thinking Child*. New York: Pocket Books, 1996.

————. *Raising a Thinking Preteen*. New York: Owl Books, 2001.

Stepp, Laura Session. *Our Last Best Shot: Guiding Our Children Through Early Adolescence*. New York: Riverhead Books, 2000.

Sullivan, S. Adams. *The Father's Almanac* (Revised). New York: Doubleday, 1992.

Willis, Kay, and Maryann Bucknum Brinely. *Are We Having Fun Yet? The 16 Secrets of Happy Parenting*. New York: Warner Books, 1997.

Winnicott, Donald W. *Talking to Parents*. Reading, MA: Addison-Wesley, 1994.

Books for Parents with a Specific Focus

The following books provide in-depth information about specific topics, problems, or techniques in parenting.

Adolescence

Elkind, David. *All Grown Up and No Place to Go: Teenagers in Crisis*. Reading, MA: Addison Wesley, 1998.

Ford, Judy. *Wonderful Ways to Love a Teen ... Even When It Seems Impossible*. Berkeley, CA: Conari Press, 1996.

Riera, Michael. *Uncommon Sense for Parents with Teenagers*. Berkeley, CA: Celestial Arts, 1995.

Steinberg, Laurence D., and Ann Levine. *You and Your Adolescent: A Parent's Guide for Ages 10 to 20*, rev. ed. New York: HarperCollins Publishers, Inc., 1997.

Wolf, Anthony E. *Get Out of My Life, But First Could You Drive Cheryl and Me to the Mall? A Parent's Guide to the New Teenager*. New York: Noonday Press, 1992.

Boys

Elium, Jeanne and Don Elium. *Raising a Son: Parents and the Making of a Healthy Man*. Berkeley, CA: Celestial Arts, 1996.

Garbarino, James. *Lost Boys: Why Our Sons Turn Violent and How We Can Save Them*. New York: Free Press, 1999.

Kindlen, Daniel J., and Michael Thompson. *Raising Cain: Protecting the Emotional Life of Boys*. New York: Ballantine Books, 2000.

Pollack, William. *Real Boys: Rescuing Our Sons from the Myth of Boyhood*. New York: Random House, 1998.

Communication

Elgin, Suzette Haden. *The Gentle Art of Communicating with Kids*. New York: John Wiley and Sons, Inc., 1996.

Faber, Adele, and Elaine Mazlish. *How to Talk So Kids Will Listen and Listen So Kids Will Talk*. New York: Avon Books, 1980.

Henkart, Andrea Frank, and Journey Henkart. *Cool Communication: A Mother and Daughter Reveal the Keys to Mutual Understanding Between Parents and Kids*. New York: Berkeley Publication Group, 1998.

Counseling and Problem Solving

Bedell, Jeffrey R. *Handbook for Communication and Problem Solving: Skills Training, a Cognitive-Behavioral Approach*. New York: John Wiley and Sons, Inc., 1997.

Berg, Insoo Kim. *Family Based Services: A Solution-Focused Approach*. New York: W.W. Norton and Company, 1994.

De Shazer, Steve. *Clues: Investigating Solutions in Brief Therapy*. New York: W.W. Norton and Company, 1988.

Jones, Alana. *104 Activities That Build Self-Esteem, Teamwork, Communication, Anger Management, Self-Discovery, and Coping Skills.* Richland, WA: Rec Room Publishers, 1998.

O'Hanlon, William H. *In Search of Solutions: A New Direction in Psychotherapy.* New York: W.W. Norton and Company, 1989.

O'Hanlon, William H., and Sandy Beade. *A Guide to Possibility Land: Fifty-One Methods for Doing Brief Respectful Therapy.* New York: W.W. Norton and Company, 1999.

Shure, Myrna B. *I Can Problem Solve: An Interpersonal Cognitive Problem Solving Program.* Champaign, IL: Research Press, 2001.

Discipline

Crary, Elizabeth. *Love and Limits: Guidance Tools for Creative Parenting.* Seattle: Parenting Press, 1994.

Curwin, Richard L., and Allen N. Mendler. *Discipline with Dignity.* Alexandria, VA: Association for Supervision and Curriculum Development, 1988.

Pantley, Elizabeth. *Kid Cooperation: How to Stop Yelling, Nagging, and Pleading and Get Kids to Cooperate.* Oakland, CA: New Harbinger Publications, 1996.

Girls

Elium, Jeanne, and Don Elium. *Raising a Daughter: Parents and the Awakening of a Healthy Woman.* Berkeley, CA: Celestial Arts, 1994.

Friedman, Sandra Susan. *When Girls Feel Fat: Helping Girls Through Adolescence.* Willowdale, Ontario: Firefly Books, Ltd., 2000.

Mackoff, Barbara. *Growing a Girl: Seven Strategies for Raising a Strong Spirited Daughter.* New York: Dell Publishers, 1996.

Pipher, Mary. *Reviving Ophelia: Saving the Selves of Adolescent Girls.* New York: Putnam, 1995.

Specific Problems

Brown, Jeffrey L., and Julie Davis. *No More Monsters in the Closet: Teaching Children to Overcome Everyday Fears and Phobias.* New York: Prince Paperbacks, 1995.

Crary, Elizabeth. *HELP! The Kids Are at It Again: Using Kids' Quarrels to Teach "People" Skills.* Seattle: Parenting Press, 1997.

Faber, Adele, and Elaine Mazlish. *Siblings Without Rivalry: How to Help Your Children Live Together So You Can Live Too* (10th ed.). New York: Avon Books, 1998.

Greene, Ross. *The Explosive Child: A New Approach for Understanding and Parenting Easily Frustrated, Chronically Inflexible Children.* New York: HarperCollins, 1998.

Hudson, Gail E. *Child Magazine's Guide to Quarreling: Help Your Children Fight Less and Get Along More.* New York: Pocket Books, 1997.

Ikeda, Joanne, and Priscilla Naworski. *Am I Fat? Helping Your Children Accept Differences in Body Size.* Santa Cruz, CA: ETR Associates, 1992.

Kalter, Neil. *Growing Up with Divorce: Helping Your Child Avoid Immediate and Later Emotional Problems.* New York: Free Press, 1991.

Paul, Henry A. *When Kids Are Mad, Not Bad: A Guide to Recognizing and Handling Children's Anger.* New York: Berkley Books, 1996.

Samalin, Nancy, and Catherine Whitney. *Love and Anger: The Parental Dilemma* (reissue ed.). New York: Viking, 1991.

Seligman, Martin E.P., *et al. The Optimistic Child.* Boston: Houghton Mifflin, 1995.

Wilmes, David J. *Parenting for Prevention: How to Raise a Child to Say No to Alcohol and Other Drugs.* Minneapolis: Johnson Institute, 1995.

Values

Borba, Michele. *Building Moral Intelligence: The Seven Essential Virtues That Teach Kids to Do the Right Thing.* San Francisco: Jossey-Bass, 2001.

Dobrin, Arthur. *Teaching Right from Wrong: 40 Things You Can Do to Raise a Moral Child.* New York: Berkley Books, 2001.

Eyre, Linda, and Richard Eyre. *Teaching Your Children Values.* New York: Simon and Schuster, 1993.

Miller, Jamie, and Cam Clark. *10-Minute Life Lessons for Kids: 52 Fun and Simple Games and Activities to Teach Your Child Trust, Honesty, Love, and Other Important Values.* New York: HarperPerennial Library, 1998.

Books for Young Children (Ages 4–8)

Berenstain, Stan, and Jan Berenstain. *The Berenstain Bears and the Trouble with Friends.* New York: Random House, 1987.

———. *The Berenstain Bears Get in a Fight.* New York: Random House, 1982.

Bernstein, Sharon Chesler. *A Family That Fights.* Morton Grove, IL: Albert Whiteman and Co., 1991.

Brown, Marcia. *Stone Soup: An Old Tale.* New York: Aladdin Books, 1986.

Burton, Virginia Lee. *Katy and the Big Snow*. Boston: Houghton Mifflin, 1973.

Cain, Barbara. *Double Dip Feelings: Stories to Help Children Understand Emotions*. Washington, D.C.: Magination Press, 2000.

Carle, Eric. *The Grouchy Ladybug*. New York: HarperCollins Juvenile, 1996.

Galvin, Michael. *Otto Learns About His Medicine: A Story about Medication for Children with ADHD*. Washington, D.C.: Magination Press, 1995.

Hamilton, DeWitt. *Sad Days, Glad Days: A Story About Depression*. Morton Grove, IL: Albert Whiteman and Co., 1995.

Lansky, Vicki, and Jane Prince. *It's Not Your Fault, Koko Bear: A Read-Together Book for Parents and Young Children During Divorce*. Minnetonka, MN: Book Peddlers, 1998.

Polacco, Patricia. *My Rotten Redheaded Older Brother*. New York: Simon & Schuster, 1994.

Reider, Katja. *Snail Started It*. New York: North South Books, 1999.

Stinson, Kathy, and Nancy Lou Reynolds (illustrator). *Mom and Dad Don't Live Together Anymore*. Willowdale, Ontario: Firefly Books, 1985.

Viorst, Judith. *Alexander and the Terrible, Horrible, No-Good, Very Bad Day*. New York: Atheneum, 1972.

———. *I'll Fix Anthony*. New York: Aladdin Books, 1999.

Books for Older Children (Ages 9–12)

Holyoke, Nancy. *Help! A Girl's Guide to Divorce and Stepfamilies*. Middleton, WI: Pleasant Company Publishers, 1999.

Lowry, Danielle. *What Can I Do? A Book for Children of Divorce.* Washington, DC: Magination Press, 2001.

Moser, Adolph. *The Emotional Impact Series.* Kansas City, MO: Landmark Editions. Including ...

> *Don't Pop Your Cork on Mondays! The Children's Anti-Stress Book,* 2001.
>
> *Don't Feed the Monster on Tuesdays! The Children's Self-Esteem Book,* 1991.
>
> *Don't Rant and Rave on Wednesdays! The Children's Anger-Control Book,* 1994.
>
> *Don't Despair on Thursdays! The Children's Grief-Management Book,* 1998.
>
> *Don't Tell a Whopper on Fridays! The Children's Truth-Control Book,* 1999.
>
> *Don't Fall Apart on Saturdays! Children's Divorce Source Book,* 2000.

Quinn, Patricia O., and Judith M. Stern. *Putting on the Brakes: Young People's Guide to Understanding Attention Deficit Hyperactivity Disorder.* Washington, D.C.: Magination Press, 1992.

Schwartz, Linda, and Beverly Armstrong. *What Do You Think? A Guide to Dealing with Daily Dilemmas.* Santa Barbara, CA: Learning Works, 1993.

Books for Teens and Young Adults

Allenbaug, Kay. *Chocolate for a Teen's Heart: Unforgettable Stories for Young Women About Love, Hope, and Happiness.* New York: Simon & Schuster, 2001.

Covey, Sean. *Daily Reflections for Highly Effective Teens*. New York: Simon & Schuster, 1999.

———. *The 7 Habits of Highly Successful Teens: The Ultimate Teenage Success Guide*. New York: Simon & Schuster, 1998.

Dower, Laura. *I Will Remember You: What to Do When Someone You Love Dies: A Guidebook Through Grief for Teens*. New York: Scholastic, Inc., 2001.

Gralla, Preston. *The Complete Idiot's Guide to Volunteering for Teens*. Indianapolis: Alpha Books, 2001.

Kaufman, Gershen, Lev Raphael, and Pamela Espeland. *Stick Up for Yourself! Every Kid's Guide to Personal Power and Positive Self-Esteem*. Minneapolis: Free Spirit Publishing, 1999.

Lutz, Erika. *The Complete Idiot's Guide to Friendship for Teens*. Indianapolis: Alpha Books, 2001.

McGraw, Jay. *Life Strategies for Teens*. New York: Simon and Schuster, 2000.

Offner, Rose. *Journey to the Soul for Teenagers*. Berkeley, CA: Celestial Arts, 1999.

Rabens, Susan. *The Complete Idiot's Guide to Dating for Teens*. Indianapolis: Alpha Books, 2001.

Shandler, Sara. *Ophelia Speaks*. New York: HarperPerennial, 1999.

Trujillo, Michelle L. *Why Can't We Talk? What Teens Would Share If Parents Would Listen: A Book for Teens*. Deerfield Beach, FL: Heath Communications, 2000.

Wilde, Jerry. *Treating Anger, Anxiety, and Depression in Children and Adolescents: A Cognitive-Behavioral Perspective*. Washington, D.C.: Accelerated Development, 1996.

Parenting Magazines

Child
www.childmagazine.com

Parenting
www.parenting.com

Working Mother
www.workingmother.com

Organizations and Other Web Sites

The American Council for Drug Education
1-800-488-3784
www.acde.org

APA Online (American Psychological Association)
www.apa.org/psychnet

Campaign for Our Children
www.cfco.org

Center for Adolescent Studies
812-856-8113
education.indiana.edu/cas

The Center for Effective Discipline, End Physical Punishment of
Children (EPOCH-USA)
614-221-8829
www.stophitting.com

Child Development Institute
www.cdipage.com

Children and Adults with Attention Deficit/Hyperactivity Disorder
(CHADD)
1-800-233-4050
www.chadd.org

Connect for Kids: Guidance for Grown-Ups
202-638-5770
www.connectforkids.org
(for kids, too)

Drew Bledsoe—Parenting with Dignity
www.drewbledsoe.com

Expert Parents
www.expertparents.com

Family.com
www.family.go.com

The Family Corner
www.thefamilycorner.com

Family Support America
www.familysupportamerica.org

Harvard Education Letter
1-800-513-0763
www.edletter.org

KidsHealth
www.kidshealth.org

National Association for the Education of Young Children (NAEYC)
1-800-424-2460
www.naeyc.org

National Center for Fathering
1-800-593-DADS
www.fathers.com

National Clearinghouse for Alcohol and Drug Information
1-800-729-6686
1-877-767-8432 (Spanish)
www.health.org
(includes tips for teens)

National Council on Alcoholism and Drug Dependence, Inc.
1-800-622-2255
www.ncadd.org

National Parent Information Network (NPIN)
ERIC Clearinghouse on Elementary and Early Childhood Education
1-800-583-4135
E-mail: ericeece@uiuc.edu
npin.org

The National Parenting Center
1-800-753-6667
www.tnpc.com

National Parenting Education Network
www.npen.crc.uiuc.edu

Parent Soup—iVillage.com
www.parentsoup.com

Parents Anonymous (PA)
909-621-6184
www.parentsanonymous-natl.org

Parent's Guide to Young Adolescents
www.courttv.com/choices/guide/index.html

Parents Without Partners International, Inc.
312-644-6610
E-mail: pwp@jti.net
www.parentswithoutpartners.org

Partnership for a Drug-Free America
212-922-1560
www.drugfreeamerica.org

Single Parents Association
1-800-704-2102
www.singleparents.org

The Ups & Downs of Adolescence: A Newsletter About and for
Young People, Parents, and All Concerned Adults
www.ianr.unl.edu/ianr/fes/ups-downs

The Whole Family
www.wholefamily.com

Games

Dragon Game (anger-sharing game)
Blue Heron Productions
Available at www.feelingscompany.com

Getting to Know You (family game)
Blue Heron Productions
Available at www.feelingscompany.com

Goose Game of Feelings (game about feelings)
Blue Heron Productions
Available at www.feelingscompany.com

Helping, Sharing, Caring Game (game to promote social skills)
Richard Gardner
Available at www.therapeuticresources.com

Let's Go Fish a Memory (game about feelings and memories)
Blue Heron Productions
Available at www.feelingscompany.com

Lifestories (encourages self-expression, affirmation, creative thinking, problem solving, and learning)
Educational Media Corporation
Available at www.educationalmedia.com

Road Rally (self-esteem game for ages 6–12)
Blue Heron Productions
Available at www.feelingscompany.com

Snakes and Ladders (game about morals and values)
Blue Heron Productions
Available at www.feelingscompany.com

Taming Your Dragon (anger-management game)
Blue Heron Productions
Available at www.feelingscompany.com

Ungame (also *Pocket-Sized Ungame*) (noncompetitive communication game)
Educational Media Corporation
Available at www.educationalmedia.com

Winner's Circle (self-esteem game for ages 8–14)
Blue Heron Productions
Available at www.feelingscompany.com

Index